Tony Greig
CRICKET
The Men and the Game

As told to David Lord
Photographs by Ken Kelly and Reg Morrison

HAMLYN
LONDON NEW YORK SYDNEY TORONTO

Published by
The Hamlyn Publishing Group Limited
London . New York . Sydney . Toronto
Astronaut House, Feltham, Middlesex, England

Copyright © Tony Greig 1976

ISBN 0 600 31925 3

Designed and edited by Charter Books Pty Ltd
Phototypeset by G.T. Setters Pty Ltd, Sydney

Printed in Hong Kong

Contents

Cricket Round the World

No matter what one thinks about cricket and cricketers, it has to be realized that the players are basically entertainers.

The principals in this dramatic comedy are undoubtedly the crowds that flock to Test matches and to many a major first-class and limited-over game. The crowds make the game what it is, and therefore I want first to pay them tribute—as well as the odd brickbat, of course. Without spectators our game would be worthless—like Frank Sinatra singing to a handful of hearers in a subway tunnel, or evangelist Billy Graham attempting to reform the lives of a picnic party on a remote hillside.

Entertainers need people, hundreds and thousands of people, before they can begin to achieve what they set out to do. And exactly the same is true of the entertainers who are chosen to be Test cricketers. The bigger the crowd, the better they perform. They are most effective when they are enjoying themselves, and, like all professional entertainers they enjoy a capacity house.

Gone are the days when cricketers just donned their creams, padded up and saw out the scheduled hours of play in the good old traditional 'play the game old chap—stiff upper lip and all that'. The public deserves more, pays for entertainment, and has a right to it. If this is a sign of the times, then believe me the times are great, exciting and a priceless experience.

Sure it's demanding. What job worth doing well isn't in that category? But it's up to the cricketers on the field and the administrators of the game never to lose sight of the fact that crowds make cricket live. There's so much satisfaction and enthusiasm when the crowd becomes involved. It rubs off on the players and the natural progression is that on-field performances improve.

I've played my best cricket on grounds where the biggest crowds have congregated in their thousands, and that's one of the reasons why one-day cricket in England has been such a huge success. County cricket has been sadly attended in recent seasons and the players haven't played exciting cricket over the three days. Of course, there have obviously been days when that bland law hasn't strictly applied, but when the one-day affairs are on, the air is electric far more often than not—just a further proof of the essential contribution spectators make to the spirit of a great game.

How crowds vary around the world! The raucous throng on the Sydney Hill, the constant din anywhere in India and Pakistan, people hanging out of trees in the magical West Indies, the knowledgeable crowds at Headingley, Leeds, Castle Corner at Kingsmead or Newlands at the foot of Table Mountain at Cape Town in South Africa, and at the home of cricket, Lord's.

If I had to choose the most electrifying crowds of all I would have to go for the Indians. They jam the grounds in their thousands, upwards of 70,000 in some cases, squashed in like sardines. Getting involved with them is a delightful experience, and thoroughly rewarding. On my first tour there under the captaincy of Glamorgan's Tony Lewis I was singled out for obvious reasons. For starters, my height of six foot seven and my blond hair were enough. They loved to roll my name around the tongue, so of course I got the 'business'.

I mean that in the nicest way, for I had a ball. After all the publicity about my South African background, I imagined that many would hold that against me, thinking from what they'd heard or read that South Africans were pretty bad people. I was very conscious of that and made a concerted effort to rid them of any doubt about my being glad to be there.

As I have always said, I'll play cricket against anyone, anywhere and at anytime. I don't worry about race, colour, or creed, and I don't believe any of those things should ever govern the mind of sportsmen. I'm a professional cricketer who loves to play the game and as far as I'm concerned politics don't enter into the sport.

I was lucky in India and I had a good start in the Delhi Test. England won and the Press gave praise, and that helped me enormously to get my message across. The one major drawback in India is the language. Playing to packed houses every Test was an experience out of this world, but I could never pick up the comments that floated across the ground from the popular section. I had to judge from the reactions and laughter what the inference was, and use sign language in return.

I really learnt about my standing with the Indian crowds when I went out to bat in Calcutta. It was obvious from the reactions of the players and the 70,000–strong crowd that they wanted me out quick smart. Chandrasekhar was bowling at the time, and bowling exceptionally well. I had no sooner taken guard when a fellow deep in the crowd started banging a massive gong—J. Arthur Rank style. It made a hideous din, to the point where it even drowned out the normal humdrum of the crowd. That was no mean feat on its own, the noise was atrocious.

I appealed to the fellow's sense of fair play, again with sign language, and he was a long way away. I went down on my knees, Buddha-fashion, signalling a plea for silence, and the crowd thought that was the greatest thing of all time. It was pure involvement. They went dilly with delight. They'd got a reaction for a start, and being really involved with a cricketer from another country was just tremendous and made their day. I made no secret of the fact that I enjoyed it too. And the gong stopped for three overs.

Slowly, but surely, I got on top of Chandrasekhar, and the gong started again. Before you could blink an eye some 20 to 30 spectators rushed from their sacred positions and hustled the man and his gong out the gate. There was no way he could ever have got back in, and I doubt that the 'ushers' would have let him if he had tried.

I was amazed. The police didn't have any say in it, for in that particular section the crowd took the law into its own hands and peace thankfully reigned.

On another occasion I was fielding on the fence, again at Calcutta, when a spectator offered me an orange. One of the major problems in both India and Pakistan is the vastly different food and its preparation, as compared to what I'm used to, but nothing too much can be wrong with an orange. The giver was delighted when I smiled, even more delighted when I accepted his precious gift and started to peel it in between deliveries. I knew I was being very closely watched by everyone in that section, and the whoops of joy as I finally broke the orange into pieces,

World Cup Final at Lord's in 1975. A typically-decked West Indian armed with maraca, whistle and rosettes on his straw hat supports his side and adds so much colour to the game

Below

Geoff Boycott *is all concentration as he plays his favourite square cut for Yorkshire against Derbyshire. Bob Taylor watches the result*

Opposite page

Ian Chappell: *more runs down to fine leg with Derek Underwood in the background*

Overleaf

Barry Richards: *Dennis Amiss watches the best batsman in the world square drive*

Sabina Park *is so typical of the West Indies; spectators on the grandstand roof and hanging out of trees*

keeping a large slice for myself and offering the remainder to the rest of the side, was a major breakthrough. They couldn't believe it, and it wasn't long before umpteen other offers were forthcoming. A little later I did want another orange, for it was a really hot and humid day, and I signalled to the crowd. In seconds the air was filled with hundreds and hundreds of oranges raining onto the playing field. It took a while to clear up the debris, but it was worth it just to see the sheer delight.

To give satisfaction as an entertainer means a lot even in England, where Englishmen are the quietest, but most knowledgeable cricket lovers in the world. Especially at Headingley in Yorkshire. There is no hill and they seem to enjoy their cricket in a quiet sort of way. But there's been a change in English crowds recently, and I put it down to the huge proportion of West Indians, especially at The Oval—bongo drums, can-banging, whistles, the lot.

Even staid Lord's, and the even more staid Long Room, have shown an emotional upsurge. When we had Australia six wickets down at lunch in the recent series, the cheers of delight and back-slapping made every one of the England side blink in amazement. All that's good for cricket, and it's even more apparent in Australia. Melbourne's huge crowds don't produce the same atmosphere as a packed Sydney ground, even though the latter is smaller. Australian crowds are by nature noisy. When their side is on top the air is electric—the call of LILLEE or THOMMO rings through your ears. At times it's deafening and a batsman must be able to switch off or be 'done' by the crowd.

There have been times when the beer has taken over around four in the afternoon and ugly scenes seemed likely. I don't mind the abuse, for I don't really believe it's directed at me personally, even though I've often been called a Pommie bastard.

That's a comment I enjoy, for it's a signal for me to get a bit back. When I'm on the boundary I get my chance to say 'Hey, get your facts right, I was born in South Africa'. If they still keep it up I'll say, 'Anyhow, you're nothing but convicts' and give them what I call the ball-and-chain sign. I tap my wrists together to denote handcuffs, then roll my hand clockwise as if I'm toying with a ball and chain. Not once has that scene brought anything but a roar of laughter and we're back on the road to all enjoying ourselves.

Unfortunately, very few Test cricketers look for byplay with the crowd. More's the pity, for the crowd does like to be involved and I sure do. You do get the odd nasty customer, but only late in the day when he's sodden. That's the time when spectators should be stopped from jumping the fence. Of course, nobody but the players and the umpire should ever be allowed on the playing surface. One of these days someone is going to dump a pint of beer on a good length thinking himself quite a performer, and that one silly act could turn a series.

I can't say I've ever been afraid of those who do invade the centre. I like to see people enjoying themselves so long as it's all in fun.

No doubt, if I ever got injured by somebody overstepping the mark, my attitude would change. I would hate to see drink banned from the Sydney Hill, for example, but one day that might just have to happen. My much-publicised love-hate relationship with Australian crowds was very fairly reported, and that was certainly the way I wanted it.

But riots are another thing altogether. People have been stabbed in India trying to get into the ground, stands have been burned to the ground. In Pakistan we had to wait a couple of hours before we could leave the dressing room. And then, as we lay face down on the floor of the bus, a brick was thrown through the window. Not one of the England side was hurt, but our Pakistani liaison officer had to receive attention. In both those countries the crowds kept up an incessant din and it got to the stage where if peace did reign you'd reckon it was all too strange.

But despite all these anti-factors, I have nothing but praise for most of those Indian and Pakistani cricket-lovers, they just live for the game. I'll never forget trying to buy some silver in Bombay. There were seven of us in the group—Mike Denness, Keith Fletcher, Dennis Amiss, Barry Wood, Mike Hendrick, Chris Old and myself—all in a small shop. The silver was magnificent, and for starters we had at least some room to move around to look. But in a few minutes the word was out—the English cricketers were in such and such a shop. Within a quarter of an hour the crowd outside had swelled to 20 deep, spilling out onto the road.

A band swung around the corner, blaring away with all the gusto of the brass. I can still hear the huge horn umpa-umparing away, then note by note droaning into complete silence. The bass drum's beat lost its rhythm and it joined the horn in utter silence. One by one the band disintegrated, peeling off to join the ever-increasing crowd who just wanted to

catch a glimpse of the cricketers in the flesh and see them far closer than at the ground. In the end we had to be hustled out the back door into cabs and back to the hotel, minus our silver.

In Pakistan, skipper Intikhab Alam tried so hard to keep a rowdy crowd quiet that he more than met his match. It was in Hyderabad, and a noisy section in the outer looked as though they were about to invade the ground in their thousands.

Inti was batting at the time and, as their hero, decided that if he went to the troubled section and pacified them, all would be well. Hyderabad's ground is dusty, and very sandy. Inti, as always, was immaculate in his creams.

Suddenly the entire section broke ranks, engulfing the pleading Inti who only wanted them to keep quiet so the Test could proceed. But his gesture got the opposite reaction and it was a very ruffled Inti who eventually wrenched himself clear, covered in dust and sand. He looked as though he'd gone fifteen rounds with Mohammad Ali.

There are dozens of stories from Pakistan and India, probably because they are both so different from home. Take the hotels for instance. In Hyderabad I went to the toilet, stood while I finished what I'd started out to do, then pulled the chain. Sadly, the plumber had forgotten to connect the downpipe to the toilet bowl and I was immediately drenched from the waist down—it gave me quite a fright.

In the same hotel I shared a room with Dennis Amiss at the end of the section. All the bedrooms were on the first floor, with the eating and reception rooms on ground level. Some of the older hotels in the area, like ours,

Greig admonishes over-zealous Indian supporters who nearly damaged the Lord's wicket in 1974

Super Pakistan: *the sign and national flag were symbolic of Pakistanis boisteriously supporting their side against Australia in the Prudential World Cup opening round at Headingley*

Bongos and beer: *Two West Indians go dilly with delight at Clive Lloyd's magnificent century at Lord's where he won the Man of the Match award in the Prudential World Cup final*

Entertainers: *Rohan Kanhai, backed by keeper Deryck Murray, throws down a bottle of bubbly to a bubbling crowd at Lord's after leading West Indies to a 2–0 win over England in 1973. A huge*

West Indian jubilantly accepts the skipper's gift and get's to work on the cork with the usual result, and the end result is sheer ecstacy

were built with a fall from left to right for drainage purposes and Dennis and I were kept awake all night as one by one our team mates used the basin or shower and water gushed through our room at the end of the line.

The dining room was something else. One night I wandered in for a meal, only to see everyone sporting handkerchiefs or napkins on their heads, looking like sheiks. When I asked what was going on I was very smartly told that the bats were out in force. The old story of how bats can get so tangled in your hair that you have to cut them out made all the boys and the Press contingent mighty jumpy.

Then someone got the bright idea to turn on the huge helicopter-like fans and did that cause some action? One by one the bats were cut down in various states of disarray, and the waiters took great delight joining in and shovelling out the remains and racing back for the next batch.

Not for one minute am I saying it was a pleasant meal, ducking as you heard another bat hit the fan, but it did provide something different. That something different makes touring a joy, providing you get off your tail and look out for the good things. They're always around and anyone who mopes his way through a major tour, no matter what the country is, is cheating himself.

For sheer joy and unabashed cricket-lovers, the West Indians are hard to beat. The Test grounds have closed signs hanging out long before play starts, and that alone gives me a tremendous thrill, for if the crowd is there showing its delight in whatever way is peculiar to that country, then it's on for young and old.

Outside the ground spectators hold precariously on to branches of trees overlooking the ground, and they have to stay there all day or lose the spot. Soft-drink sellers make a small fortune wandering up and down the street outside the ground, catering for the tree-dwellers who instal a pulley system specially for the purpose. How they attend to nature I'll leave you to work out, but the ones I felt sorry for were those whose branches gave way.

In many ways West Indian crowds can be just as volatile as their Indian or Pakistani counterparts. During the Port of Spain Test against West Indies last tour I ran local hero Alvin Kallicharran out off the last ball of the day. That on-the-spur-of-the-moment action almost precipitated a riot, even though I was well within the laws of cricket.

Derek Underwood was bowling from the far end toward the pavilion with Kalli the non-striker. I was fielding at silly point when Bernard Julien patted the last ball of the day past my right hand in the direction of extra cover.

I covered some ground, picked up the ball and in one movement threw at the bowler's end stumps as I saw Kallicharran heading down the wicket. Umpire Douglas Sang Hue had not called over or time so he had no option but to give Kallicharran run out, on appeal. As it turned out, all Kallicharran was doing was heading for the dressing room, content that the day's play was over.

By some stroke of luck his name wasn't taken off the scoreboard. If it had been, I'm quite sure all hell would have broken loose right there and then. Somehow I doubt if many really knew what had happened anyway, but once the word got around

thousands of very irate West Indians were calling for my blood.

Of course there was another aspect to this, for I was very conscious of being South African-born. Many papers had blown this up, and I had taken particular care to show that I was Tony Greig, and no racist from South Africa. But I'm proud of my South African birthright, proud to be able to tour the world with everyone knowing my South African background.

In anti-South African countries such as the West Indies, India and Pakistan I feel the same as I do in any other country where I am a guest. But if I can, in any small way, break down the animosity towards the country of my birth, I welcome the chance with open arms. So you can see that the Kallicharran incident could have had serious repercussions. After a rather hurried conference between our manager Donald Carr and local officials, Kallicharran was reinstated for the next day. It was a prudent decision, even though Kalli admitted he was in the wrong and that Sang Hue was quite right in giving him out.

That night was one of many that deeply impressed on me the personality of Garry Sobers—the man who first gave me my chance in big cricket when he and Sir Donald Bradman invited me to tour Australia in 1971–72 after the South African tour to Australia had been abandoned. Sobey believed in me, and for that I will be eternally grateful to the greatest all-round cricketer the world has ever seen.

But on that hot and muggy Port of Spain night I admit I was terrified. Sobers sat with me and we talked until 10 that night, while there were still hordes of angry West Indians outside wanting my hide.

Sobers was asked by one of our own pressmen what he thought of the whole affair and he said that if the incident wasn't cleared up quickly, life would be so intolerable for me that I would be better off going home, just for my own safety. To that pressman's shame he quoted Sobers as saying, 'Greig should be sent home'. Nothing was further from the truth, and that alone could have sent the frenzied mob to riot.

But thanks to Sobers and the time he spent with me as we waited for the anger to die a bit, we were able to leave together for the England side's hotel. I shudder to think what would have happened if their own cricketing God hadn't been so thoughtful, hadn't personally insured my safety. I was still wary the next morning, but the hoots and jeers turned to cheers when Alvin and I walked to the centre and shook hands. From that moment on all was forgotten, and I returned to my usual tricks on the fence forgiven for having the audacity to run out their hero.

Kallicharran added only five to his overnight 140 in a great innings, and I spent the rest of the tour accepting, more than just a little warily, drinks offered from the fence. For those who have never tasted West Indian rum, I can assure you that it has the kick of ten mules, hardly the sort of drink to be swallowed during a Test match, or in any other match for that matter. But I had some leeway to make up, and I smilingly accepted the numerous offers, rolled my eyes in what appeared to be ecstacy but in truth was sheer fear, nodded to the giver and quietly walked in with the bowler while letting the lot dribble

Hero worship: *Deryck Murray is mobbed by countrymen after leading West Indies to a great win over Pakistan in the Prudential World Cup at Edgbaston 1975*

First: *Michael Angelow became the first streaker at Lord's, the home of cricket*

down onto my shirt. Usually it was so hot the evidence was gone before I turned again towards another offer. Had I swallowed all those drinks I would have been carted off smashed out of my mind long before the session was finished.

In beautiful Barbados, the birthplace of the great Sobers and countless other West Indian cricketing giants, the crowds were immensely keen, tremendously thick shoulder to shoulder, and a delight to play in front of.

For that Test we couldn't get close enough to the ground in our bus, so we walked to the outskirts of the ground, climbed over the outer fence, and carried all our gear across the field, much to the delight of the milling throng. In Trinidad you can't walk anywhere without seeing dozens of 'Tests' being played with all sorts of equipment anywhere from back lanes to open parks. It's a constant surge of cricket, cricket, cricket. No wonder the West Indian Test teams are full of such effervescent players, who all started in that same fashion.

South Africa is very different and it is necessary to look at their situation from two points of view—before South Africa was boycotted, and now. If a national side was to tour there now, every ground would be packed every day. That's how much they are yearning to be accepted.

Right now the situation there is very dangerous although they have made a huge effort. I know, as does everyone who is fair-minded, that South Africa has moved in the right direction by trying their level best to set the coloured question right, offering to help finance non-white sports.

If anyone had asked me five years ago if it would be possible to play in a multi-race competition in South Africa I would have looked at the questioner with blank amazement. But for the past couple of years I have played in the international double-wicket tournament at Johannesburg that has included local coloureds Edward Habane and Duncan Stamper and last year Pakistani's Mohammad Ilyas and Younis Ahmed and West Indian John Shepherd. That's another huge step in the fight for recognition, but what's really needed is encouragement. If encouragement isn't forthcoming—as it hasn't been—then the South Africans can be forgiven for thinking that they are doing the right thing. But nobody is telling them anything, and some real encouragement would speed up the process of correction.

Surely nobody expects South Africans to simply change their whole life pattern overnight and conform. In all fairness, a tremendous amount has been achieved in a short time and it's up to some country to publicly recognise this and send a full touring side to the Republic.

What I would like to see is an experimental national side tour, inviting all the other major Test-playing countries along as observers. Then it could be put to a majority vote, after having seen at first hand what the real situation is in South Africa. That would be a fair method. At present it's all against South Africa, a case of guilty until proved innocent, and I don't think that will achieve anything worthwhile for anybody.

Once representatives of every country have seen the real South Africa, they could spell out what they wanted the Republic to do. The International Cricket Conference would then be fully armed with on-the-sport information from every member nation, which would be a far better position for that governing body to be in, rather than awkwardly and rather reluctantly wiping South Africa off the international cricketing slate.

After all, the sporting problem isn't really the issue. The issue, in the end, is one man one vote—that's what everyone wants, that's world opinion. It could well turn out like the French Revolution. A little bit here and there won't be good enough, the whole thing will have to change. But there is no way that South Africans can give away their security just in five minutes. There have got to be steps in that direction, slowly and purposefully; it can't all be pressure from one side.

The crowds are dying to turn up in droves to see Test cricket on some wonderful grounds in South Africa. The superb Wanderers Stadium at Johannesburg is something somewhere between Melbourne and Calcutta, full of life and with a magnificent view from anywhere on the ground. The Press box there has to be seen to be believed, perched up as high as you can get, looking right down on the players and yet ever so close. That's a great spectacle. But if a touring side went there right now, the crowds would be just crazy for South Africa, there would be only one team in their eyes, whether the crowd was black or white.

Newlands, quieter, but a beautiful ground set among glorious trees, with the magnificent Table Mountain in the background as its permanent guardian, is the Lord's of South Africa. Port Elizabeth and Kingsmead have their own particular features. The latter is more like the Sydney Hill, on a sloping grassy bank with a marquee in the corner—Castle Corner. The same words of wisdom pour forth from that area as in Sydney and from the same sort of beer-loving crowd.

It's such a shame that for the time being, or however long it takes, the sport-hungry South African spectator has to sit tight and gain his only solace from the first-class, purely domestic, Currie Cup competition.

New Zealand, in other ways, is in the same boat. Touring sides breeze through, usually at the tail-end of an arduous Australian tour, just too jaded to start the ball rolling again under different conditions. And with no alcohol allowed into the ground, the crowds are quieter and less willing to become involved.

So touring New Zealand isn't like touring anywhere else in the world. It's a beautiful country and the people are kindly hosts, but it's in the centre of the field that it counts from the players' point of view. Of course, finance is a governing factor, but every endeavour should be made at the administrative level to give New Zealand players more international competition. On our last tour there we played against less than twenty players in five matches—hardly the sort of encouragement to be given to promising youngsters.

So that's cricket the world over. I've been fortunate to play in other places such as Sierra Leone, Singapore, Bangkok, Hong Kong and Sri Lanka, and have a great deal of pleasure and take away many happy memories. But it's the memories of players that I've played with and against that I want to relive now—the best players in my decade of first-class cricket, and what makes them great in their own departments.

Alvin Kallicharran: *a classic cover drive from the little West Indian*

Below

Found the gap. *Dennis Amiss takes another two runs during his 183 against Pakistan at The Oval in 1974; keeper Wasim Bari and fieldsman Sarfraz Nawaz*

Overleaf

John Edrich. *John Steele looks on as Edrich plays a familiar back cut during the Benson and Hedges Cup final at Lord's*

The law steps in at Lord's during the Prudential
World Cup final when Australian Alan Turner was
impeded on the ropes.

Electric: a major game at Lord's is something to
remember

What Makes the Greats

Ability, temperament, concentration. These are ingredients that make up the balance of any player—the greats have all three. It doesn't matter what era we talk about, though I'll stick to mine when it comes to examples.

Ability is a must. Some are born with it, others work to better it, but there must be something there in the beginning to work with. The natural batsmen like Garry Sobers, Barry Richards and Graeme Pollock are all freeflowing strokemakers chock full of natural ability. Yet with their very brilliance, they can also be unpredictable, inconsistent.

Then take a batsman like Geoff Boycott, or even John Edrich. Their natural ability is way below that of Sobers, Richards and Pollock, but for sheer consistency and predictability they take some beating. Their performance shows the hours and hours they have worked diligently on their game.

Whereas the free-flowing strokemaker can, and often does, hit good balls screaming like tracer bullets to the fence, the Boycotts and Edrichs of this world chip away at the bowling, keeping well within their own range of shots. This range is very limited and there might be touchy words from those spectators who like to see the ball hit hard and often, but every team vitally needs stabilising batsmen. It's all very well to have a team of dashers, but dashers rarely fire together. Even more importantly, they don't win enough games and if you don't go out to win, what's the point of playing?

So my advice to those who criticise the Boycotts and Edrichs of this cricketing world is to pay them the due they deserve in their own way. After all it's the runs on the board that win the game. I'll take a Boycott or Edrich century in 300 minutes any time, preferably both in the same innings. Then I know England will get at least 450, and it's pretty hard to lose Test matches with scores like that.

Both these batsmen will take a back seat if one of the dashers is on the move, but they are there to pick up the pieces when something goes wrong. And the strokemaker's unpredictability rarely comes to the player who plays within his special limitations.

Some players don't use their ability, even when it's natural. A perfect case in point is Australia's Gary Gilmour. When he's in the mood I doubt if there's a better Test all-rounder in the world. He bats in a hurry, and can really take any attack apart, no matter how good it is. He bowls superbly, on his day. I've seen only the great Sobers and West Indian Bernard Julien move the ball away in the air as Gilmour can, and that's a major plus factor in so few left-arm medium-pacers.

In fielding Gilmour can do the lot. He can field close in and take some fantastic catches off his own bowling, yet he has one of the best and strongest arms in the game. But like all naturals he is unpredictable, far more so than anyone else in international cricket at this moment.

Yet temperament plays just as big a role as ability in the make-up of the great player. It applies in all departments of the game, but probably stands out more noticeably among bowlers—to their credit. Speedsters like Dennis Lillee, Jeff Thomson, Mike Procter and John Snow all show their temperament in different ways.

To start with, with the exception of Thomson, these men are ferocious-looking bowlers. You can bet anything you like that if

Gary Gilmour: *determination here, but not always consistent*

they are hit for four—and Heaven help anyone who hits them for six—they will be back at the batsman with a vengeance. Thomson doesn't really let you know what he feels, or is thinking, but the net result is the same.

Spinners haven't that fierceness about them, naturally enough, and in their own way their temperament must be so controlled that they can come back at a batsman after being smashed around the ground. The ones who can come back make the grade. Those who do it best become great. Of course, the same can be applied to batsmen, fieldsmen and keepers as well. If the crowd sets about a batsman with slow handclapping, he must be big enough inside to shut the noise out and get on with his work.

Personally, I welcome slow hand-clapping from two angles. If I'm batting it makes me even more determined the bowler isn't going to gain an advantage from anything other than his own ability. If we are bowling, as captain I try to use the extra benefit handed me by the crowd and pin the batsman down even more so that the handclapping gets louder and louder. I reckon that gives me an extra fieldsman or two, and a better than even chance of getting the batsman out. I encourage the crowd to keep going.

Many good players have been upset by the crowd, and that's why they have never, nor will they, ever become great. How often have you seen a fieldsman miss one, then another, then misfield the ball all day? That's purely temperament. By the end of the day all he wants to do is find a hole and crawl into it. He's annoyed with himself, the crowd has given him hell, and there's nowhere for him

Frank Hayes *is another Gilmour leg-before victim, as were Keith Fletcher and Alan Knott*

Eddie Barlow, *a non-stop bundle* of energy

to hide. The same can be said of keepers, in exactly the same way. But in both cases those

For all that hardy bunch of cricketers, concentration is vital, and it's mighty hard to concentrate on every ball bowled, especially if it's a long day in the field and the spinners have worked hard and a lot of overs have been bowled.

I can't imagine anything worse than squatting and standing, squatting and standing for six hours in places like Karachi, Calcutta, Bombay or some of the hot spots in the West Indies. Keeping is a hell of a job, and the greats of the keeping world get my greatest admiration.

The keeper has to be sharp all day, every ball. The old saying, catches win matches is so true, and the glovemen are generally in the thick of things. But although concentration applies to batsmen, bowlers and fieldsmen as well, at least there are moments when you can shut off, whereas the keeper is constantly on the move taking returns, backing up or whatever.

But the greats can hold their concentration for most of the time, far more than those who are graded good players. Now there are players such as Eddie Barlow and myself who are not great players in the true sense of the word. We haven't got that natural ability I've mentioned before, but we've utilised every aspect of the game and make a point of making sure that we are involved. While both of us are ordinary bowlers and batsmen, we have become recognised as being very forceful cricketers. We apply ourselves with less ability, but because of our total involvement with bat and ball, and anywhere in the field, we can make up some of the leeway on the recognised greats.

23

So much for ability, temperament and concentration—but without enthusiasm most of it's not really worthwhile.

Test cricketers show their enthusiasm in different ways, but I know that if I don't really show how enthusiastic I am, then I get nothing out of the game. Barlow's the same.

Spectators make a really big thing out of players showing their enthusiasm. Personally, I make up for the ability I lack in this way. I've got to believe in myself all the time.

If I'm bowling to Sobers and he plays and misses, I'll do a somersault. But, on the other hand, if Sobers and Richards were as enthusiastic as Barlow and myself, we'd never get them out. Not that I'm saying either of those great players isn't enthusiastic—they just don't show it.

It goes without saying that fitness finally touches off what makes players great. It never ceases to amaze me how Lillee keeps going, how Alan Knott and his keeping colleagues last out a day—I could go on and on naming players. If you're not fit there's no way you can concentrate for long periods, and if you don't concentrate you're history. You'll get out with the bat, get smashed all round the park with the ball, and drop catches.

Some are fanatics like Knott, constantly on the move. Others, like me, just look after ourselves, making sure we can last six hours a day for each day of a Test. Anything less fails to let you give your best. So any player must take pride in what he's doing—pride in the way he plays and pride in the way he presents himself. And on top of all that, pride in what he is doing for cricket. This, in turn, naturally breeds a lot of jealousy.

When Boycott and Richards clash in the Yorkshire-Hampshire game, for example, neither really wants to see the other perform well. Basically, each is trying to do better than the other, and recognises the other as a great player. A head-to-head duel, if you like, and to win such a battle means a lot to either player.

I've had my battles with Ian Chappell on the field. Neither of us will give an inch, but we pride ourselves in believing, rightly or wrongly, that we can do honest battle, though individually we must win.

what they do, and, more importantly, take pride in how their team mates perform. Of course, there are players whose only pride is in what they do themselves, while the rest can make their own arrangements. That attitude isn't good for cricket. It is too selfish for the game to benefit. Boycott has been placed in that category, but that's unfair. He takes great pride in how his Yorkshire youngsters perform, and the proof was in how well the County did in 1975. It was Boycott's leadership and drive that did that.

With the bat, it's a different story. He grafts runs for Boycott, knowing full well that unless he gets hundreds, the side could be in trouble. Yet even then, Boycott is all the time 'fathering' his younger and far less experienced batsmen along, while he dictates proceedings. Yet in a head-to-head with, say, Richards, it's a fight to the death and no holds barred.

So these are among the many and basic ingredients of a great player. From here on in all those factors will become abundantly obvious as we move through the greats of my time.

My many faces *when I crack New Zealander Dayle
Hadlee in the ribs at Trent Bridge in 1972. Wonder,
exult, clap, ask, worry, assist and claim a wicket*

John Edrich, *not natural ability, but all-out
dedication*

I like to keep up the pressure. *If the crowd
starts slow-clapping, to me that's an extra
fieldsman or two*

The Blitzmen
The Great Fast Bowlers

Blitzmen, that's a fair term for some of the greatest sights on the cricket field.

Crowds flock to the ground to see a fantastically fast bowler go through his paces. Batsmen who have to withstand all that goes with it cannot be said to enjoy the same feeling, but the great blitzmen are certainly a magnificent spectacle and they really draw the crowds.

Once again I'm talking about the blitzmen of my era. I can't honestly compare Lillee, Thomson and Roberts with, say, Harold Larwood, Ray Lindwall, Frank Tyson and Wes Hall. I try to steer clear of making comparisons like that.

Take the front-foot bowling law for starters. In the days of Larwood and Hall they operated under the back-foot law that placed no restriction whatever on the front foot. Providing the back foot landed roughly in the same position every ball, a blitzman could easily stretch a further six inches or so closer to the batsman without being called.

As it was, all those great blitzmen were up to four feet over the batting crease, and were therefore four feet faster through the air as compared to their present day counterparts. So there is no way, absolutely no way of fair comparison. Even though it's always interesting to hear older spectators making their own claims about Larwood's speed, for example, I won't be drawn into that sort of discussion because I'm not in a position to claim any sort of authority there. But I have no hesitation in naming my five blitzmen as Dennis Lillee, Jeff Thomson, Andy Roberts, John Snow and Mike Procter, and not in any particular order, for they all have something different to offer as international cricket stars.

I won't even compare them individually for speed, for once a bowler has hit the high velocity these five have reached most of the time, he falls into the same blitzman category without a murmur from batsmen or spectators. When you think about it, what's the difference between 89 and 92 miles per hour? When it's all boiled down they're plain, straight-out quick. There are other factors that must be taken into consideration, such as movement in the air or off the wicket, bounce, line and length, ability to fire under different conditions, the will to come back at a batsman after taking some stick.

All these factors make a great blitzman— and these five great bowlers have mastered almost every one. There are others I'll mention later that on their day, or under special circumstances, have matched my top five. But over a long period Lillee, Thomson, Roberts, Snow and Procter have no peers in my era.

I say over a long period because an innings, or even one Test match, isn't a fair criterion for an honest assessment. Take Lillee and Thomson for example. Lillee invariably has the wind, Thomson has been used against it as well. On a given day or match one might be firing more than the other, but over a series or two the truth is known, for consistency is a hallmark of the greats.

There's Lillee, a great bowler, a great competitor, a great cricket thinker. I have the highest admiration for the Australian. The way he fought back from a serious back injury deserves the utmost praise. For Lillee has had two careers, the one prior to his back injury, and 18 months later another, starting with the last MCC tour to Australia. Lillee had enough

Jeff Thomson, a doddle run up, and then a perfect delivery at express speed

How's that? *It takes a strong umpire not to be intimidated by such a ferocious appeal*

Opposite page

Dennis Lillee, *all aggression, all the time. Alvin Kallicharran watches the result*

in him to overcome a massive setback and again be a force—and is he ever a force! In the terms of my top five, Lillee must be the fittest man around to carry out his role, and he does a lot of hard work.

But Lillee's major asset is aggression; snarling, vocal, and calculated to upset a batsman. That's over and above tremendous ability, a ferocious approach that I reckon has caused the downfall of many top batsmen even before he lets the ball go, and his very physical appearance—hair all over the place and drooping moustache.

Aggression just pours out of Lillee, that's the way he plays the game and I would never dispute its worth. Even when he is on the defensive, such as the 1974 Sydney Test when Australia wrapped up the Ashes, the fiery West Australian barks out his feelings in no uncertain manner.

I had the delight of hitting Lillee on the elbow, probably one of the most painful areas of the body. I say delight, for I had been on the receiving end of many searing Lillee deliveries and even though at my medium pace I could hardly return the same venom, striking Lillee gave me a lot of pleasure because I knew nothing could be broken, with the possible exception of some pride, even vanity.

But not for Dennis. As he vigorously rubbed his elbow and spat out unprintables I was warned for intimidation by umpire Tom Brooks. While I was 'speaking' with Brooks, little Keith Fletcher wandered from slip to pick up Lillee's bat, which he'd hurled away in anger at being hit. As 'Fletch' offered the handle to Lillee, he couldn't resist the remark,

'It's high time you got one back'. That was too much for Dennis, who called Fletcher for everything, repeating earlier threats that plenty more were in store for the Englishman. Fletcher withdrew the bat, throwing it back onto the ground. By now Lillee was hopping mad and it was all I could do to stop laughing aloud.

At the end of the day I took a bottle of beer from our dressing room in to Lillee, asking him how the elbow was. Still glaring, then smiling, Lillee said, 'OK Greigy, today was yours, but I'm not likely to forget it—and there are plenty more days to come yet'. That's what I like about Dennis Lillee, you always know where you stand. I take great delight in baiting him, knowing I'll get an instant reaction, and maybe just break his concentration a little.

That's why I bowled him a bouncer in the first Test at Brisbane. Like many class bowlers Lillee loves to bat, and fancies himself too. He was starting to look a nuisance when I asked skipper Mike Denness if I could bowl at him, knowing full well I was going to let him have it, bouncer and all. Lillee was 15 at the time I really let a bouncer go, using all that Brisbane nip off the wicket available, and believe me, there was plenty.

As the ball climbed towards Dennis' head he threw everything to the wind in a desperate lunge for safety. The ball clipped his glove and went down the legside as I gave my appeal all I had. Off went Lillee, angry at the bouncer and angry at the decision because he didn't believe he'd hit it. He had to walk past me to the dressing room and I knew, right there and then, I was on a

One for me. Headingley 1975 and I cut Dennis Lillee through the gully for four, yet he's still ultra aggressive

Opposite page

Dennis Lillee, *the great Australian speedster with an equally great action, watched in earnest by another Australian, now England Test umpire Bill Alley*

promise. Between clenched teeth Lillee said, 'I'll catch up with you'. He meant it, and I had asked for it.

When I came out to bat in England's first innings we were in strife at 4-57, and Dennis reminded me that I'd had my go, and now it was his turn. Back he went way beyond his normal mark and in he came like a train. His whole attitude was belligerent, aggressive. His eyes were glazed and he gave that ball everything on a mighty quick wicket. It scorched past my nose as I withdrew, and it was still climbing as it cleared Rod Marsh. With two bounces it thudded into the fence in front of the Clem Jones Stand for four byes. Almost immediately I heard the thump, thump, thump of Lillee's follow-through and I looked back towards the Australian who was standing only feet away with hands on hips, cursing me.

That was the pattern for my entire innings, but in the long run I believe I had a points decision, especially when I raced towards my first Test century against Australia by hopping into Lillee with a series of rather cheeky back and square cuts for four.

But this was the start of a head-to-head duel that will always be felt when Lillee and I are opposed. Yet underneath all the snarls and aggression I will always admire him as a truly great blitzman, and that feeling was deeply embedded during the Rest of the World tour in 1971–72 and conclusively proved for me when the Australians toured England immediately afterwards. On that tour Lillee broke the Aussie Test record with 32 wickets in the series to really make the top grade.

For Lillee, as a great cricket thinker, can adapt his bowling to the conditions. As he has the ability to move the ball away in the air and can shrewdly change pace with seemingly little change in action, Lillee can overcome unhelpful conditions. He can in fact switch the entire situation around to work to his benefit. That takes a lot of thought to fire, and a lot of ability to put into practice.

Off the field I've found Dennis Lillee to be the perfect gentleman, and I rate him as a good friend. Dennis, Ross Edwards and myself, with our wives, dined out during the second Test in Perth and nobody would have guessed that during the day Dennis and I had been at each other hammer and tongs. It's all very well to dish it out on the field, but it's just as vital that at the end of the day Lillee and I can talk about the play, be it good or bad. We've knocked over quite a few bottles in either dressing room during the three series we've been at each other, and I have thoroughly enjoyed it all on and off the field.

That's easy to do when you respect someone. A lesser man than Lillee would have turned it up after suffering such a bad injury, but he went a step further by trying his hardest to make himself into a batsman when he couldn't bowl. For one full club season in Perth Lillee captained his side as a batsman, striving with the same application as he did with the ball. But events have shown that his determination again to be a bowling force has reaped rich rewards. Dennis Lillee must have a deep feeling for the game to have overcome so much. When I first saw him during the World XI tour of Australia I felt he was just another strongly-built quick who could well be another five-day wonder. Even after he'd sliced through us in the second international at Perth I didn't really think he could be a

great. There seemed to be nothing special about him. But by sheer dedication and application he went from strength to strength. The Perth debacle was on the quickest wicket I've ever seen, and it was tailor-made for Lillee, or anyone who had speed through the air. What Jeff Thomson would have done the same day, I shudder to think.

That was all part of Lillee's apprenticeship. Today he's fully qualified to be among the greats, no matter what the era. For D. K. Lillee is a sensible, good-thinking, honest-working fast bowler—no doubt about it, Lillee is great.

So, too, is Jeff Thomson, but in so many different ways. There's nothing aggressive about Thommo either in his approach to the wicket or in his attitude on the field. But the net result once the ball leaves Thomson's hand can be just as devastating and in many ways even more lethal. For Thommo has a plus-factor that none of the other four blitzmen possess—he's so completely deceptive.

The first time I faced Thomson was at Brisbane in the first Test last summer. I had been rested from the warm-up game against Queensland, and had therefore missed the chance to have a good look at him. Three successive balls went by without my making contact, so I asked John Edrich if he'd take Thommo for awhile until I'd settled in. I told him I was having difficulty picking up the line, as Thommo was so deceptive. Edrich was happy to oblige, providing I took Terry Jenner. I replied that would be a pleasure, for I love facing T.J. and John doesn't fancy the leg spinners.

That was my century innings, so Edrich certainly did me a favour early in the dig as there's little doubt in my mind that I would have lost out if I had been left to sort Thommo out at that stage, by myself.

In the second innings Thommo had worked out that what he called a 'sandshoe crusher' was the best chance to pick me off early. I'd scored two when Thomson ripped in a searing yorker that forced me to lift my foot as it slanted into the batting crease and careered through to send my leg bail some 15 yards back towards Marsh. Full credit to Thomson for succeeding in his plan, but no marks for trying to repeat the effort every time since then. I should be very grateful to Thommo for trying again and again, for in the process he's bowled me any number of over-pitched deliveries or half-volleys, and those runs were gratefully accepted, thank you Thommo.

But I don't for one minute want to give the impression that Thomson doesn't think about the game. He does, in his own way. He's unlike Lillee in that he rarely gets involved in field placing, leaving that to his captain. All Thommo does, in effect, is take the ball and get on with the job, and that's all he has to do. True, his direction is often astray, but that only adds to his striking power, for if he has no idea where the ball is going, then the batsman has no chance trying to read him. So Thomson's inaccuracy works for him, not against him. In every other way Thomson is a blitzman to be respected, and not only because he's awfully quick. The way he gets the ball up so quickly, and quite often it's vicious, makes him a deadly striker. I don't care how good a batsman is, this type of delivery makes you keep a very wary eye on the fellow. Anything less only courts disaster.

Frustration. *Jeff Thomson winces as a chance from David Steele goes astray when Ashley Mallett, in the gully and out of picture, could not hold a hot catch and the rebound didn't reach a diving Rod Marsh*

Occasionally Thommo makes the ball dip in, and he can move it off the seam away to the slips. That is commendable too and a difficult ball to deal with under any circumstances. So Thomson has his own peculiar personal attributes and what great attributes they are. He's been rightfully described as a 'slinger'. His huge wind-up at the point of delivery follows an easy approach over about half the distance used by Lillee. Therefore Thomson doesn't take as much out of himself, especially with his doddle run-up that fits a medium pacer. That's the first way Thommo is deceptive, for it's hard to believe any bowler can give so little in the beginning, and produce so much at the end. But Thomson has a fine action when he puts it all together where it really counts.

Yet, again unlike Lillee, Thomson hasn't ever said a word to me in the middle. I haven't tried to bait him at all, purely because it would be a waste of effort. It's not that I don't want to upset him for fear of wearing the result, but because the exercise simply would not achieve anything. All I bait a bowler for is to distract him from his job and Thommo is utterly impossible to dent. The worst I've seen him do is give the two-fingers sign to the crowd if they're baiting him, hang his head to the left with his hands on hips if he's disappointed, or snap his fingers and wave his arms across his body if he's all over the shop in direction. Compared to Lillee these actions are powder puff, yet that's the way Thommo plays his cricket. Underneath, he's just as fierce a competitor as Lillee, but simply not so demonstrative about it. They are a magnificent combination and Ian Chappell has been fortunate to have them both firing so well

with that equally great medium pacer Max Walker in support. Walker has been shamefully under-rated since he began his highly successful Test career against Pakistan three years ago.

But back to Thommo. To me, he has a classic action. The way he whips everything into a frenzied delivery made me first of all think the opposite. But on reflection, after having watched him more closely, I rate Thommo's last three strides as classical for him. That's his physical situation, peculiar to him alone, and the connoisseurs rate him highly. Again he's vastly different to Lillee after delivery. Whereas Lillee quite often follows through to within a whisper of the batsman, Thommo stops dead after delivery, as if he's run smack into a brick wall.

So his main assets are blistering but deceptive pace, and the ability to make the ball climb off a good length. He can bowl you a few balls that really don't do much, and all of a sudden, without any indication in his approach, Thommo can rip one into you that's ever so quick. That's why he's such a great striker, a perfect shock bowler. Whereas Lillee might bowl a tight line on the off stump because the wicket isn't helpful, Thommo will still be trying to make the ball climb over the keeper's head. Not that that's such a bad thing, because Thomson is a shock bowler who doesn't need to be subtle. Frankly, if I was captaining Thomson that's the way I'd use him—short spells of sheer speed and just let him run amok as best as he knows how. Ian Chappell obviously used Thommo in much the same way, for the speedster is strong, and can bowl for long spells with little loss in pace. Experience will teach him that his speed

Garry Sobers. *The great left-hander lofts the ball over mid-off during a big innings at Edgbaston*

Overleaf

All Power: *Clive Lloyd climbs into a sweep during his superb second innings century against Australia at Melbourne, 1975*

Mike Procter, *hair flowing, wrong-footed and fearsome*

through the air will always hold him in good stead—he doesn't have to make the ball climb all the time to be dangerous.

Thommo is lucky in that so many wickets in Australia are conducive to his type of bowling. In England, India, Pakistan and the West Indies Thommo won't, and didn't, get much help. But once he overcame his front foot problem in England, he was again an awkward customer, again just through the air. For his sake I hope he doesn't change anything. He tried to run in faster towards the end of the English tour but he can forget it.

Off the field Thommo is rarely seen. In the dressing room he's good company, but all too often he has a few quick beers, then he's gone. One could be forgiven for thinking Thommo a rowdy, tough, aggressive bloke, especially after all the stories about him. But that's not the case. He's quiet and not a big extrovert. Rarely does he involve himself with the crowd, unless they set about him. Occasionally he does, and when that happens Thommo is great value. Everyone loves him, especially in Australia, but deep down he prefers to let the game happen, rather than make it happen.

On Thommo's arrival in London he was told that the wickets were going to be slow, and he would have to struggle to make the ball bounce. To which he replied, 'Who said the ball had to bounce anyway?' That was a great comment and one of the reasons why nobody baits the big Australian. Although it wouldn't get you anywhere, Thommo is just as likely to slip you a hand-to-head ball if he was riled enough. So, on all counts, why bother—it could be a very painful experience, even if it 'slipped'. Thommo can bowl a ball three yards outside off stump, who's to say he couldn't bowl a beamer?

I have the highest admiration for Thommo nevertheless. He's done so well in such a short time, and words will never hurt him. The same can be said of West Indian Andy Roberts. I tried him out in his first Test, tried to get at him to mess up his concentration but, like Thommo, it had no affect whatever. I tried everything, yet Andy just kept plugging away at express speed, not even recognising that anything had been said. That was in the West Indies, a place not renowned for assistance to pacemen, yet Roberts was the one to watch. I was amazed at how he could make the ball bounce in the batsman's half of the wicket, a sure sign of a good bowler. In the interim, Andy Roberts has proved a great bowler under any conditions. In those early days he was a change bowler, not a frontliner, but like Thommo he had the ability to make the ball bounce from nowhere.

The difference is that Roberts is accurate all the time. He's worked at it, because he surely wasn't like that at the start. His attack was either half-volleys or bouncers—what we call up or back balls. All you had to do was get out of the way of the bouncer, then wait for the half-volley and smash it away. Now he's somewhere in the middle, a great fast bowler who's really fast.

Approach-wise Andy falls in between Lillee and Thomson. He hasn't the all-out aggression of Lillee, nor the doddle of Thomson to the wicket, yet he leaves you in no two minds that he's after you.

Despite the aggression, Roberts is a very quiet man, almost to the point of being embarrassed he's there at the top. County

Keith Boyce, *perfect balance and at times as fast as anyone in the world*

John Snow, *an ideal bowler for any youngster to copy*

Andy Roberts, *perfect balance, perfect rhythm*

Peter Lever *can let a few rip*

Sarfraz Nawaz, *bowls within himself*

Opposite page

Bob Willis' hat trick *during the John Player League game for Warwickshire against Yorkshire in 1973. First to go was Richard Hutton, then David Bairstow and finally Phil Carrick; all bowled*

Andy Roberts, *quiet and quick*

Vanburn Holder *can be really fast*

cricket has brought a bit out of him. As a player with no malice whatever, it's a joke around the Hampshire dressing room about Andy Roberts' 'black book'. The players tried to get Andy geed up a bit, and suggested that he kept a note of those batsmen he wanted to catch up with for any reason whatever. There are very few names in the 'black book', but once you're in there, you're in for the high jump.

It's not hard to see that this world of cricket must seem huge to Roberts. He was brought up on the tiny island of Antigua, and in the space of a few months was the talk of the cricketing fraternity all around the globe. Quite rightly too. Any fast bowler who can do what he did in India and Pakistan on their frightfully slow wickets deserves all praise. And to crack the record with   wickets in India was further proof of just how great a bowler he is. There's no doubt in my mind that he'll get better.

I'd hate to play against a World XI side that would have to have Lillee, Thomson and Roberts as their pace attack. That would be sheer hell and mighty painful as well. There'd be no respite, and even if the games were played in Bombay where the wicket isn't conducive to speed, the mere fact these three are so fast through the air would still make them a threat. If it was in Perth, it would be cricketing mayhem.

Mayhem is a word synonymous with John Snow. I don't think there have been many fast bowlers who on their own have swung a Test series, but Snowie did just that in Australia in 1970–71 under Ray Illingworth's captaincy to regain the Ashes. Snow was dynamic in that series. I know him well, for we both play for

Sussex, and when I see that blue ring appear around his mouth I wait for Snow to blow. He can get mighty angry, even though he doesn't really say too much. But when he does, his other preoccupation of being a poet comes into good effect. Snow hasn't a black book, but he does have the memory of an elephant. One of his pet hates is a batsman who continually plays forward.

Very softly, but with any amount of feeling, Snow will say, 'Look I would suggest it might be a good idea if you got on your back foot, and stopped sticking that big pad at me'. Sounds pretty mundane, but believe you me any batsman with any cricketing brains at all will take heed, or know full well he'll pay the full consequences with a searing bouncer around the heart. Even a number 10 could incur the wrath of J. Snow. He has been termed a 'heart bowler', one who primarily aims his deliveries to rip into the heart area. For batsmen, that's one of the toughest areas to protect, and Snow has claimed many a wicket as the ball flew high off a frantic wave of bat or glove.

Hampshire's keeper Bob Stephenson has a nightmare time against Snowie. The most seemingly innocuous things can upset Snow, as Stephenson found out first time up. Stephenson takes guard with his left hand on the bat, and his right hand down behind his right leg. I've never seen anyone else do it anywhere in the world. Snow had captured a bundle this day on a quickish wicket, and wasn't in the mood to waste any more time, even though he was running down the hill. At full pace Snow approached the crease, only to see Stephenson in this peculiar position. Snow stopped, thinking the batsman wasn't

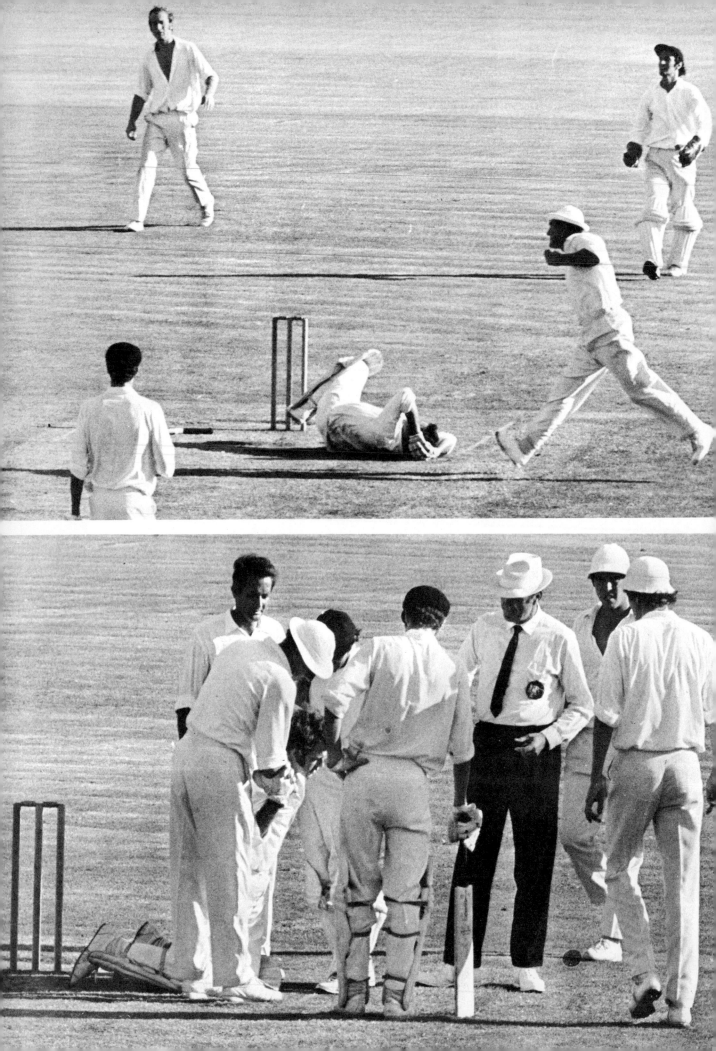

The infamous 1971 incident when John Snow felled Australian Terry Jenner at Sydney. It eventually led to England captain Ray Illingworth leading his team off the field. Jenner goes down, Illingworth rushes in to assist and helps Jenner to his feet

A jubilant John Snow takes another wicket as Ian Chappell waits anxiously for the result of a leg-before appeal.

ready, and trudged back to his mark.

When it happened a second time, Snow sighed rather loudly, went back to his mark and called out if Stephenson was ready yet. Away went Snow, for the third time, and again it happened. Snow snapped.

Stephenson, playing his first game, couldn't work out what was wrong with England's best fast man—must have lost his run or something, but why get angry with me? Poor Stephenson. Every season when he comes in to bat, Snow wants the ball, he wants to knock his head off—that blue ring is most noticeable. Middlesex's Mike Smith is in the same boat.

Snow is the ideal bowler for any young paceman to copy. He takes little out of himself on the way to the wicket and he bowls right off the point of his toe to gain maximum height. That high action enables him to get tremendous lift off a good length and he can move the ball in the air and away off the wicket. In all, John Snow is a magnificent bowler and a good cricket thinker. Yet he thrives on a contest; these days it needs something extra to make him really feel competitive in County cricket.

Geoff Boycott brings out the best in Snow. I well remember an incident at Hove against Yorkshire. Snow rates Boycott highly and vice versa, so automatically there's a contest. So long as the conditions are equal, or roughly so, then it's on. This day Boycott batted first, played out a maiden from Snow, then squirted the first ball of the second over through the slips towards third man. In a rather un-Boycott like gesture, he tapped Snow on the knee as he touched down at the bowler's end. Snowie's immediate reaction

was to kick Boycott's back leg from under him, sending the Yorkshireman into a double somersault. Boycott was very nearly run out as he completed what should have been an easy two runs.

Both complained to the umpire about a friendly Boycott gesture that backfired, especially for Yorkshire, and it was really on. The next ball hit Boycott between the shoulder blades and went over the keeper's head for four leg byes. The ball after that broke his wrist. Both were lightning fast deliveries in Boycott's half of the wicket and unplayable. Said former England left-arm spinner Don Wilson, 'We should never bring Boycott to Hove if Snowie's playing, it stirs him up too much and we are all likely to get killed'.

That was in 1969, Brian Close's last season with Yorkshire. Close followed Boycott, and I've never seen anyone take such a deliberate pummelling. I'd heard all about Close the hard man, the man who took Wes Hall on the body. This day Snow was at full bore, yet Close took four successive and sickening blows to the chest without offering a shot. He was out hit on the elbow, the ball rolling behind his body and onto his wicket.

That was blitzman John Snow, a man quite capable of changing his whole approach if the conditions warranted it, such as at Lord's last season with a career-best eight wickets. Anyone who read that could be forgiven for thinking Snow must have been quick. In fact Snow virtually bowled slow off-spinners, looping the ball over the top of the sight-screen into the trees—most of his wickets were bowled.

John Snow has been often criticised, most

Sir Garfield Sobers, *a classical action, but when he wanted to be, ever so quick*

of the time unfairly. He does his thing his way. I've had no problems with him at Sussex and now with England, because I made a point of understanding him. Strange but true. Sure he can be temperamental, sure he can be hard to handle, but it's well worth working out what makes him tick, because he's a truly great fast bowler. And to those who blast him for not trying all the time, do they honestly expect a man of Snow's pace to bowl flat out every game?

Lillee and Thomson have the advantage that they usually play far less major cricket than any County player and can therefore afford to go hell for leather every game. Theirs is not a seven-day-a-week, six-month-of-the-year stint. Roberts, Snow and Mike Procter cannot risk burning themselves out—who can blame them for pacing themselves? If the wicket is slow and there's a sparse crowd Procter automatically comes into this category because of his thundering pace. His now famous wrong-foot action belies extreme pace, but when you think that Procter isn't much slower than Lillee, Thomson and Roberts—or the Snow of the early seventies—yet can move the ball in through the air so far and so late, then that's one hell of a bowler.

Procter takes some picking up from the hand. This wrong-foot action really means a delay in the front foot coming through, giving him a windmill-type delivery very similar to Australia's 'Froggy' Thompson of the early seventies. With his long blond hair streaming in the breeze, Procter gives out all the aggressiveness of a Lillee and he runs about the same distance. At the end of his run up he's going like the clappers, following through to the batsman, and he's not

backward in saying a few well-chosen words. He had more than just a few for Gloucestershire against Sussex. The man on the end of it was Sussex's opening batsman Ken Suttle.

It was Procter's first County season and here was this strongly-built tearaway back some 50 yards almost running off the ropes. Unbeknown to Procter, his firm friend and teammate David Green had conned Suttle into a pint of beer for every time Suttle could stop Procter on his fearsomely fast approach, but they had to be consecutive. 'Let's get the young lad going', he said.

In roared Procter. About ten yards out Suttle backed away and asked for the sightscreen to be moved. Back trudged Procter almost out of sight as Suttle turned to Green at bat-pad and said, 'That's one pint'. Procter turned, was just over halfway to the wicket, and again Suttle pulled away, this time complaining about something in his eye. Green obliged, seriously taking out his handkerchief to find the trouble.

By now Procter had either walked or run somewhere around 250 yards, but had yet to let the ball go. Suttle settled as Procter let rip a series of expletives, and for the third time tore in. Five yards out Suttle again pulled away saying, 'I can't see, I can't see'. Procter exploded, Suttle turned to Green and said, 'That's three pints', while Green couldn't contain himself anymore, falling to his knees in peels of laughter.

'Hey, Proccy,' shouted Green, 'Ken was on a pint for every time he does this. Three times he's done you, three times'. A startled Suttle said, 'No, no!', and did Procter give him the business. Three stoppages were followed by three scorching bouncers that were no balls,

Andy Roberts *bowling to Ian Redpath at Melbourne in 1975; nagging accuracy and express speed*

Opposite page

Ready to go. *Dennis Lillee winds up in England 1972 as he comes to umpire Tom Spencer and non-striker John Edrich*

Keith Boyce graphically captured on his follow through as Notts' Mike Harris looks on

Dennis Lillee *in harness with a serious back injury that threatened to ruin his career in 1973. His return as a fast-bowling giant says volumes for his courage*

so in the end Procter had run in twelve times to complete his opening six-ball over. At the end of the day David Green parted with his three pints, but Proccy demanded and got three to match.

It's a shame Procter has had such a limited Test career, for there's no doubt in my mind that his figures would have been astonishingly good. But with South Africa on the outer, that's it for Procter, unless there's a change very shortly. A serious knee injury has forced him to concentrate more on batting of late, but in his prime, what a great bowler.

So they are my five blitzmen, though there are others, who on their day and when the conditions are right, spasmodically fall into the same bracket.

Keith Boyce heads that list. There have been times when he's bowled exceptionally fast, but not often enough to be classed a true blitzman. He's as strong as an ox, has a tremendous bouncer, but doesn't quite measure up in pace to the other five.

Garry Sobers had moments when he really let them fly, and swung it both ways with a beautiful action. Boycott didn't want to face Sobers, he'd prefer to tackle Wes Hall and Charlie Griffiths. Sobers was so much a striker with a classical action. Had Sobers not been such a great batsman, and just concentrated on his bowling, he would have been something right out of the box as a bowler. Take the case of the Sobers-Lillee tangle at Melbourne during the World XI series. Sobers had copped plenty from Lillee, he knew they were in store, but he felt it was high time he dished one out. The Melbourne wicket was as dead as usual, but Sobers nearly took Lillee's head off with a scorcher, it was really quick. 'You're not the only one who can bowl those',

was Sobers' quip and Lillee got the message.

Peter Lever and Vanburn Holder have let a few rip that rate with the best of quickies. Bernard Julien is deceptive, yet can also slip a few swift ones through. One day at Lord's Bob Willis was so much faster than normal—as fast as anyone I'd seen—that the slips went back ten yards from where we first were. That's a hell of a long way, and that day Willis was really on the boil. Alan Knott said during the spell that Willis was the fastest he'd ever kept to, but this was a oncer, though it proved he could do it under certain conditions.

Chris Old showed enough in India on unresponsive wickets to indicate he'd strike a high pace note somewhere along the line, but he's never come up to those expectations and has always bowled well within himself.

Pakistanis Sarfraz Nawaz and Asif Masood come into the same category, joined by New Zealand's Richard Collinge. Most of these chaps make up for lack of pace by making the ball move, there's more time through the air to do so. The Indians have nobody who could remotely fit into the category, while South Africa's giant Vintcent van der Bijl, a massive six-foot eight, can be very bouncy and slippery at times. But none of those mentioned in the occasional bracket can live with Dennis Lillee, Jeff Thomson, Andy Roberts, John Snow and Mike Procter. They are truly blitzmen, even with an old ball—it doesn't matter if there are chips out of it.

Bouncers are the perfect example. My five top men can still part your hair, the rest would make the ball sit up softly enough to put away with ease. My dictionary states 'blitz' as lightning, sudden or surprise warfare. That's Lillee, Thomson, Roberts, Snow and Procter to a tee.

The Run-Makers
The Great Batsmen

When one thinks of the game of cricket one thinks basically of a battle between bat and ball. That sounds rather obvious, but let's not forget that a bowler has first go with the action —he's the one who has the first chance to dictate the trend of the game.

So when a run-getter is classified as great, it's because he has consistently forced the bowler into the background through his own brilliance. Therefore he's not only taken over the running, but he has dominated play to such an extent the bowler is either replaced or the entire attack is pulverised and beaten. So to be classed as a batting great is more than just an achievement. It takes a genius, one who has picked up the basic principles of batting early in his career and with his natural ability has put it all together brilliantly.

The greats can make a mockery of the game. If I was asked to choose one man that I would not want to bowl to it would be South African Barry Richards. To him goes my highest praise and my deepest sympathy. Praise for the fact he's the greatest batsman I've ever seen, sympathy because such a batting genius has only played four Tests and those were as long ago as 1970. Even worse, there's only the faintest chance that he'll ever play another Test. I didn't start until 1972 and now have played in forty-two official Tests for England. I could never rate myself anywhere near Richards' standard.

What a tragic waste of talent! In England, spectators can see him turn out for Hampshire, Australia saw him for one season in South Australia, New Zealand for a double wicket competition. But without Test matches as a goal, Richards at times looks to have become bored, though he still remains a great player.

The same applies to Graeme Pollock, Mike Procter, Eddie Barlow, all first-rate Test players. They are as good as most players in the world, but their toast is dry with little butter and no jam. All players need motivation and long, dreary days without that Test match atmosphere must sap their motivation.

So how good is Barry Richards? I make him my number one on many counts, not least of which is the fact that I've never seen him in trouble for any length of time. He has so much time to play any bowler no matter how fast, and very seldom gets struck out, mainly because his bat always seems to do the hitting. At some stage or another I've seen all my greats pushed to stay out of trouble, never Richards.

He plays brilliantly all round the wicket. If you bowl anything short outside the off-stump you know as soon as you let the ball go that it'll crash into the fence around the point area. If it's short enough it may well end up over the mid-wicket fence, pulled with a vengeance seldom seen. Both these shots are hit like tracer bullets.

To make matters worse, Richards seems always to know where the field is set and adjusts his shots accordingly, flicking or blazing them through the gaps. I have often wondered if it would be possible to keep him quiet with thirty fieldsmen, maybe then he'd come back to the field. I have studied Richards for years, trying desperately to find some flaw. I thought I'd performed the impossible a couple of times, but now even that avenue is closed.

Richards had a habit of picking the ball off his toes and depositing it over the square leg umpire's head, lobbing it some five to ten yards inside the fence. Twice when I was

Barry Richards. *The best batsman in the world shows how perfect footwork and balance make him the greatest*

playing for Eastern Province in South Africa we picked him up there. Not any more. To him, batting is a doddle. If he gets bored he just wanders outside the leg stump and cuts you unmercifully for four, past or backward of point, only because he picks up the ball so quickly. So there's no way any bowler can say, 'Leave Barry Richards to me today and I will keep him quiet'. Once he gets the bit between his teeth he crashes you to all parts of the ground, seemingly effortlessly.

It's sad that it takes a television camera team to get the best out of Richards. As the trucks roll onto the ground for a limited-over game you can bet Richards will get at least 50, often more. Hampshire team-mates who bat in the lower order say, 'We have no hope of getting a hit today', and rarely are they wrong. It's sad, for week in week out Richards plays before a handful of spectators, gets out, returns to the dressing room and switches on the television to watch the likes of me playing for England against Australia to a packed house at Lord's. It's hard to imagine the pain that must cause.

Playing with Richards has done many players the world of good. Take West Indian Gordon Greenidge. When he first came to Hampshire he was so raw, all brute strength. Opening the batting with Barry three to four times a week has made him a Test player.

This is where the situation is so incongruous. Richards cannot play Test cricket because of apartheid, yet he opens with black-as-ebony Greenidge, and takes any number of catches for another West Indian, their champion blitzman Andy Roberts. Yet Richards hasn't a hope in hell of playing in the West Indies, nor Greenidge and Roberts in South

Africa. But the three of them are close friends, sharing the Hampshire dressing room daily. So who can blame Barry Richards for feeling frustrated, even cheated.

For the aspiring young cricketer, Richards is an ideal batsman to copy. He lifts the bat up straight, technically everything is so correct. He's not like the West Indians who literally wind themselves up and into a shot, everything is smooth, calculated and timed to perfection. He plays the game hard, far harder than the casual outward appearance he gives.

In Australia he picked up the nickname 'Glue', because he never walked. He always believes the umpire's job is to adjudicate, and leaves it entirely to him. So he stays glued to the crease until he's given out. Many non-walkers get mighty angry if others don't walk. Not so Richards. I remember a Currie Cup game in South Africa, playing for Eastern Province against Natal, where I literally drove three big nicks into the keeper's gloves on the way to making a scrappy 12. Richards was at slip, knowing full well each time I was out. But all he said was, 'Crikey Greigy, it must be your day today'.

So that's Barry Richards, great batsman, great competitor, under-rated off-spinner and very safe slips fielder, everything done with consummate ease.

The greatest compliment I could pay Geoff Boycott is that if it was possible to mould the natural brilliance of Richards and the utter dedication and concentration of Boycott, there you would have the perfect batsman.

I've always described Boycott as a self-made player. Obviously he has ability, but not the natural flair of Richards. What has made him one of the great players is his dedication to

Graeme Pollock, *all power, placement and perfect timing*

Another Boycott injury. *This time he collides heavily with West Indian keeper Deryck Murray. Garry Sobers looks aghast and captain Rohan Kanhai moves in to assist at Edgbaston 1973*

Colin Cowdrey. *A century in his hundredth Test and a youthful looking Ian Redpath, Eric Freeman, Ian Chappell and Bob Cowper acknowledge a great feat*

and absolute love of batting, possibly more so than any other batsman of my time—and that is a compliment to the man for the work he must have put in.

His life revolves around batting and there's no doubt he's run-hungry. I have never seen any other Test batsman make 130, go back to the dressing room for a glass of squash, mop his brow and then ask, 'Is there anyone who would like to have a bowl?' Just the thought of it makes me tired, but that's Geoff Boycott all over. During the day there might have been some shots he'd played he wasn't happy about and it took him three hours before he reckoned he'd ironed out the faults so they wouldn't happen again.

On another occasion Boycott was 200 not out overnight and arrived early at the ground for a two-hour session at the nets before the start of play. As luck would have it, Boycott was out quickly that day and all that did was make him even more determined. So it was back to the nets for another two-hour stint.

People tend these days to be very critical of Boycott and his attitude to the game. He has been described as a selfish player, but that is really only the outward appearance of his dedication to run-getting, just as Richards has been often described as too casual.

Boycott's defensive technique is almost perfect. That is the main reason why he has been hit so many times, getting well behind the line. Having played most of his cricket in Yorkshire on slower wickets, it is little wonder Boycott is an expert cutter of the ball. Unlike Richards, Boycott can be contained because he is a percentage-no-risk player. I know that if I bowl six balls at Boycott just outside off-stump and moving into middle off, he will

play the lot straight back to me. So he can be kept quiet, but his patience is so unlimited that once you stray off line he will despatch you for four. In the meantime, he will just patiently pick up his ones and twos and utterly frustrate a bowler to such an extent that sooner or later Boycott will get the ball he has waited for and quickly pounce on it.

The only time Boycott really ran into trouble during his heyday was on inconsistent-bounce wickets. Whereas other great batsmen have been able to adjust, Boycott has got himself into such a groove that he is not as adaptable as the more adventurous batsmen. For example, he would never do what I do, such as cut the rising ball over slips' heads. That has brought me a lot of runs, but obviously there is a risk involved. I am prepared to take that risk, Boycott is not. Therefore, on good wickets I am saying that he is the best player there is. There's just no way you can get him out. Take the 1970–71 England tour to Australia, where on good wickets Boycott was the one the Australians really wanted to see out. Since then, Boycott has been plagued by inconsistent wickets and has been hit so many times, breaking bones in his fingers, wrists and arm, that his performances recently have been well below the high standard expected of him. Frustration is something Boycott just cannot live with. That has been borne out by his unavailability to play for England.

I believe that deep down he truly wants nothing more than to be Test captain. That's natural and the way he goes about trying to secure that coveted job is Boycott's own business, but it is a shame he cannot see his way clear to wear the England cap. He is too

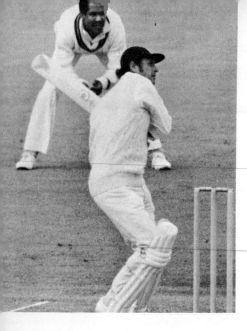

Geoff Boycott *is a study in concentration closely watched by Garry Sobers at Edgbaston 1973*

Opposite page

Rohan Kanhai, *adaptable and effective*

good a player just to play County cricket and it is little wonder that last season he performed so well to lead Yorkshire into second place on the County table. The self-made player such as Boycott reacts far more to failure than anyone else, especially if he cannot adapt to a different set of circumstances. For Boycott eats, sleeps and drinks cricket and is very conscious of his average, for after all that is the proof of his endeavour in the centre and there must be times when he thinks he is not the player he used to be. Whereas Richards would shrug off a failure and say there will be another day, Boycott feels very deeply about failure to the point where it hurts.

There have been many times when Boycott has been unfairly treated by the press. For example, in the final Test at Port of Spain in Trinidad, where England squared the series one all, I got all the credit by taking 13 wickets in the game, but without Boycott's 99 and 112 we would never have been in a position to force a win. But Boycott was hardly mentioned in despatches. This was the tour when Boycott openly criticised captain Mike Denness and this received wide publicity, for the press has been only too ready to swoop on Boycott.

I honestly believe that if Boycott had played his cards right over the last couple of years he would now be captain of England. However, I am England's captain and I make no bones about it, I want Geoff Boycott back in the England side. If he remains as dogmatic about not playing again for England, then I have just got to accept it and let him go about his own business. For Boycott is a fanatic about everything he does on and off the field. In many ways he is like Alan Knott. Both chomp through bottles and bottles of honey, never touch sugar, both constantly exercise, although Boycott does not go through the never-ending range of calisthenics Knotty does on the field. Boycott will never tour India because he has a phobia about being taken ill out there.

Even though Boycott is a very complex character, he is possibly best summed up by two occasions over recent years. First was the Test against India at Manchester when he was twice dismissed by the friendliest opening bowler in Test cricket—Eknath Solkar. Boycott was stunned by his first innings dismissal, but he was so shattered when Solkar repeated the effort second time around late in the day that Boycott was still sitting in the dressing room long after most of us had left. The second was on our last tour to the West Indies, when Boycott, as a tour selector with the manager, Donald Carr, Denness and myself, agreed to bat at number four to stiffen the middle order. Out of sheer habit, Boycott padded up from the start and wandered around the dressing room fully prepared to bat, but that did not eventuate until midafternoon. He was like a caged lion, muttering and chatting to himself just to relieve the tension. He has always opened and found his new position very strange, but he did that for the sake of the side.

I have got nothing but the greatest admiration for Geoff Boycott as a player, and I am hopeful that in the near future his problems will be resolved, for I have no doubt that if they are it will be in the very best interests of English cricket.

The greatest innings I've ever seen was

Opposite page

Thommo and friends. *Ace speedster Jeff Thomson with a packed Brisbane crowd in the background for the first Test against West Indies in 1975. The non-striker is Lawrence Rowe, umpire Tom Brooks and fieldsman Terry Jenner*

Mike Denness *agreed with Donald Carr, Boycott and myself that Boycott bat down the list*

played in Australia by that master left-hander Garry Sobers for the World XI against Australia. Those were 254 princely runs from the left-handed genius.

We'd been having a pretty lean run on tour, and I vividly remember Sobers sitting beside me at our weekly Saturday evening organised by manager Bill Jacobs, and saying, 'If I have to win this game all on my own, I'll win it'.

Here I was, a young cricketer just starting to make the grade, listening to the greatest all-rounder of all time making a big statement and then going right to do just that. I believe only Sobers or Richards could make such a statement, then carry it out to the letter. Other great players could say it and mean it, but not have that glorious gift to follow it through.

I will be mentioning Sobers time and again throughout this book, for his brilliance shines through in every facet of play. That day in Melbourne will live forever in my memory. He literally smashed the Australians all over the ground with a mixture of copy-book stroke play and some Sobers-invented gems, all of which found holes, many bouncing some fifteen yards back off the concrete wall. Sir Donald Bradman has seen so many great innings that for him to class Sobers' 254 as the best he'd ever seen gave it the official stamp of approval.

When The Don speaks, everyone listens. Quite right too! I must admit I still shake a little in his presence, mainly from embarrassment. As a young man I was brought up on Don Bradman and Vera Lynn, mainly because my father was in the RAF a long way from home and Bradman was his cricketing idol. The World XI tour to Australia was my first major tour. The last thing my father said to me as I was about to start my big-time career was, 'If you meet Sir Donald, listen and absorb'.

We arrived at Adelaide at five in the morning and a little fellow wearing a cardigan and dark glasses came over the tarmac and introduced himself. Hylton Ackerman was with me and neither of us caught his name. However, he was kind enough to invite us for coffee at the airport. We sat down and were soon joined by two others, Phil Ridings, and Australian selector, and Darby Munn, secretary of the South Australian Cricket Association.

We started talking cricket and I made the biggest blunder of my career. I turned to the little fellow in the dark glasses and asked, 'Do you have anything to do with cricket around here?' He was great and gave nothing away until Sobers came into the room. When I heard Sobers greet Sir Donald I would have been very happy if the earth had opened up and swallowed me. My father read about the incident in the press after Sir Donald had verified the story. Dad didn't write to me for two months!

I tell this story because Sir Donald and Sir Garfield have played major roles in my career. I often wonder what would have happened without their support in those very early days. I'm grateful Sir Donald was so understanding that fateful morning. Just as I was grateful, indeed honoured, to receive a telegram from Sobers just before my first Test in 1972 against Australia. It read, 'Good luck, I'll be watching' and is still one of my treasured possessions.

So if you get the impression through this book that I owe a lot to Garry Sobers, you're

Roberts v McCosker. *Victory for Roberts at Brisbane 1975 as McCosker edges the ball to Deryck Murray. Slips men are, from left, Gordon Greenidge, Lawrence Rowe and Alvin Kallicharran*

Below

John Snow, *perfect follow through, Bevan Congdon the non-striker*

Greg Chappell. *A great shot from a great batsman*

quite right. For the man was unbelievably brilliant. But like all people who have that touch of magic, Sobers had moments when he was at least mortal. This was borne out even more by the fact that he was a true calypso cricketer, born and bred in Barbados, born to play the cricket the West Indies are renowned for. Therefore the natural unpredictability wasn't far from the surface.

When Sobers was on the boil, only the incomparable Richards was his master. They had more than just that genius touch about them. Neither wore a thigh pad, so rarely were they hit. On the rarest of occasions Richards may put a sock in his left-hand pocket if there is someone really swift around, Sobers never.

Sobers' windup into a shot was all West Indian—a windmill preamble to a stroke chock full of power. I still rate Richards the more graceful, Sobers tended to mix his shots. Yet both are devastatingly effective.

Whatever Sobers did before the shot was played, when ball met bat it was in perfect position with the blade showing the full face, and from there Sobers played every shot from the latest late cut to fine-finest leg glance. Being a left-hander helped. I've always believed good left-handers look better than good right-handers, Sobers even more so.

Strangely enough, Sobers never tried to read the ball in the air, preferring to work it out off the wicket. That was typical Sobers. Just play it as it comes. That's why so many class bowlers have hung their heads in disbelief. The bowler may have pitched a ball a foot outside off-stump and reasonably well pitched up, only to see it hammered to the boundary in front of point. Next ball, pitched

in exactly the same place, could well disappear between mid-on and mid-wicket. How do you bowl to a man like that? And Richards is the same.

Such is the drawing power of Sobers that even when he could play a bad knock of 30 there would still be four or five shots that stick in the memory. And how many times have you seen him drive like all fury with his front foot up in the air. It's only after the ball has gone screaming to the boundary that the foot comes down.

I have never seen Sobers sound off on the field, with that one exception when he nearly tore Dennis Lillee's head off in Melbourne. Sobers had told us in the dressing room before play started that Lillee was his, that it was high time someone gave him back a head hunter. 'And it might as well be me', was Sobers' comment and he did just that. Lillee went white as it scorched between his chin and throat at a searing pace.

Searing pace to the fence with effortless ease best describes the many shots belonging to South Africa's Graeme Pollock. For a start Graeme uses a bat that weighs over three pounds. Compared to the average bat, his is like a telegraph pole. And his timing is so spot on that these two factors combine to rocket the ball to the fence, with a fair percentage well and truly over it. When Pollock and his brother Peter joined the World XI side in Australia halfway through the tour, we travelled to Newcastle, north of Sydney, for an up-country game.

I had been telling Pakistan's Zaheer Abbas and tiny Indian Sunny Gavaskar all about Graeme, for they had never seen him play, yet had heard so many stories about him. When

Gordon Greenidge *can afford to smile, for he's learned so much from opening the batting at Hampshire with Barry Richards*

Typical Sobers: *concentration, application. An admiring Alan Knott is the witness*

Dennis Amiss, *just missed a world record*

he went out to bat this day, these two settled down to watch one of the world's greatest players in action. The opposition's fastest bowler was in full cry, with his tail up after just claiming a wicket.

First ball Pollock leaned into and hit on the rise. It shot off to the fence like a bullet, no trouble at all. I was watching Zaheer and Sunny closely, and they started to yabber away with eyes bulging. Next ball was fractionally shorter, again just outside off-stump. Pollock started to move forward, changed his mind and went on to the back foot and pulled. Zaheer and Sunny couldn't believe it. Pollock seemed to have hours to change his mind. The result? The ball soared over the mid-wicket fence and out of the ground. An effortless shot.

Both shots were so typical of Graeme Pollock. When he came back to the dressing room, both Zaheer and Sunny were in raptures and wanted to feel his bat. Sunny could hardly lift it, Zaheer not much better, for it was a brute of a thing, yet it was so effective in the hands of Pollock—the first man to use such a heavy blade.

Poor Richard Hutton. At that stage of the tour he'd been really in the wars, hardly scoring a run or taking a wicket, and being the son of legendary Sir Leonard Hutton wasn't an easy path to tread either. So Hutton asked Pollock if he could use his massive bat rather than his featherweight blade that had brought him no luck at all. Richard played forward defensively to the first ball he received, and immediately called 'No!'

To his utter amazement, the ball sped through the covers for four. Hutton looked at his bat and turned to the dressing room to catch Pollock's eye, he just couldn't believe it. The result was that Richard Hutton took three of Graeme's bats back to England—imagine the excess baggage!

Strangely, Pollock's not a strong man, in fact he's got quite frail arms. But he doesn't exert himself, relying on superb timing and letting the trudgeon do all the hard work. Length doesn't mean a thing to Pollock. He can pick up a ball of short or full pitch and drive it anywhere.

Yet he can be contained. Pollock will invariably let a bouncer go by without offering a shot. He relies heavily on the drive and pull, not playing a hook until late in a big innings when he has every bowler whipped, then it's still rare. So you know that if you bowl him a bouncer you will have a dot in the scorebook. At least that does keep him quiet. And he reacts. He doesn't like watching a perfectly-timed shot cut off by a deep fieldsman, so he can be frustrated.

Pollock is at his best batting to a normal field, not deep mid-off, deep mid-on, point on the fence. Pollock loves to smash away and gain a just reward. He's often said it's easier to get runs in Test cricket than anywhere else. In Tests, wickets are better prepared and field placings are more regular, with a couple of slips and a gully to medium pacers or better. But in club or Currie Cup cricket in South Africa, Graeme Pollock is the star, so the field is ultra-defensive to give him one run and attack the other batsman. Often there isn't even a slip.

While I rate Pollock as brilliant, a player who so easily goes about the business of getting runs, I can't rate him in the Richards-Sobers class, and he's obviously a vastly

Lawrence Rowe, *the first with a double and single century in his Test debut*

Another six. *Clive Lloyd crushes into a lofted on drive watched by Alan Knott*

Man of the match. *Clive Lloyd accepts my vote after crashing an undefeated 73 in the 1975 Gillette Cup final for Lancashire against Middlesex at Lord's*

Glenn Turner, a *solid, no risk batsman*

Alvin Kallicharran; *ever so keen to get on with it*

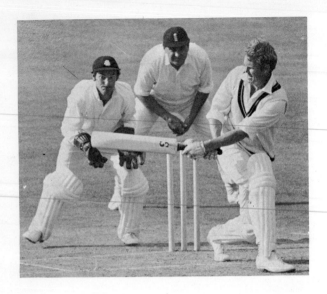

Graeme Pollock *sweeps Don Wilson during another century innings, this time for the Rest of the World against England at The Oval in 1970. Looking on are keeper Alan Knott and Colin Cowdrey*

Opposite page

Ian Chappell *seems to have decapitated Bob Woolmer at Lord's in 1975 sweeping me for four, a typical Chappell shot*

different player to Boycott. For Graeme Pollock can be frustrated, can be contained, can be niggled out.

Richards makes a mockery of the game by taking bowlers apart, Sobers does give you a slight chance with so many unorthodox shots, but neither can be frustrated, contained or niggled. Yet with all three on the go, brother, it can be hell!

My final two batting giants are Clive Lloyd and Greg Chappell. Lloyd, the immensely strong West Indian wielding a bat slightly heavier than Pollock's and made heavier with four grips; Chappell, the frail-looking Australian with elegance, timing and yet untapped talent.

Lloyd doesn't take bowling apart, he massacres it. Basically he likes the front foot, but unlike Pollock, Lloyd can hook. Of all my top batsmen, Clive Lloyd is the most explosive. Those fortunate enough to see his 102 against Australia in the Prudential World Cup final will vouch for that. Yet he's done it time and again. I remember bowling to him at Edgbaston on a good wicket when Lloyd played for the Rest of the World. This day Lloyd and Sobers were in full flight and it was a harrowing experience.

But one shot from Lloyd will particularly live in my memory. We'd taken the new ball without success and the crowd went dilly with delight as Lloyd smashed the living life out of a ball from me that was just short of a length. It screamed past my head before I had time to react, the umpire dived for safety and the ball climbed from a height of about six feet from where I stood frozen to the spot to only twenty feet as it smashed into the press box on the perimeter of the ground.

I just had time to turn around to see pressmen diving for cover. Had the ball gone a couple of feet higher, the scribes would have been covered in shattered glass. That proved the force of the man, it just went flat all the way through sheer brute force.

In that same series at Trent Bridge we had worked out that because Clive hooked in the air quite often, it was worth the calculated risk of trying to buy his wicket early with that shot. David Brown was given the job of bouncing Lloyd, three times an over. The first Lloyd hit with a half top edge and it just carried for six. Unlucky. The second he didn't quite middle, but it went thirty yards over the boundary for six. The next one Lloyd did middle and it disappeared out of the ground. Some calculated risk!

That's where Lloyd is so terribly dangerous. His brute force overcomes a mis-hit, it can still go for six, whereas any other player would be caught near the boundary.

Yet in 1971 fears were held for Lloyd that he might become a paraplegic. At Adelaide, playing for the World XI against South Australia, the cat-like Lloyd dived in the covers to catch Ashley Mallett. Only Lloyd could have got there in the first place. When he grasped the ball in both hands, Lloyd was parallel to the ground in full flight. As he came earthwards, Lloyd tried to roll to one side before he hit the ground. When he did he just lay there in terrible pain.

It was a sickening sight. Here was this superb athlete crying out 'My back, my back', with tears running down his face and in intense pain with crushed vertebrae. For days Lloyd's future wasn't known, but it seemed certain his cricket career was finished.

Thank God that wasn't so. Today Clive Lloyd thrills millions around the world with his superhuman feats as batsman and fieldsman and thoroughly deserves to be classed among the greats. He's been so dedicated. And the main reason why Clive Lloyd the batsman is now so great is that he doesn't premeditate his shots like he used to, he plays them all on their merit. Gone are the slaphappy days, although naturally, like all West Indians, there's still very much of the calypso cricketer in him, though more restrained. Now he's Test captain, I have no doubts he'll be an even better player, for he will have more responsibility.

The same could well apply to Greg Chappell. Here is a man who is immensely strong on his legs, yet has a sound technique overall. If there is a flaw, we in England suspect it's outside off-stump and we look for the nick to slips. This is almost always natural in players who are great on-side batsmen. But on his day Chappell will get runs, no matter where the ball pitches.

Out of all the greats I've mentioned, Chappell compares more with Richards than the others. He's that sort of player—everyone compares him that way anyhow, although I say without hesitation Richards is the better player. Aussies disagree with me in that, but Chappell is the best player in Australia and he will get better. He's a magnificent front-foot player who can move onto the back foot and whip you through mid-wicket with consummate ease.

Just to qualify my leanings towards Richards as against Chappell, I very much doubt that Richards could go through a tour of England and fail so consistently in Test matches as Chappell did last tour. Chappell really had a terrible tour. Take away the one score he did get, and he'd averaged under 10, which for a player of his class was unbelievable. Some Test teams are going to pay for those failures for a long time.

I commend Chappell for the way he's worked on his game. When he came to Somerset in 1968 there were no indications he would turn out to be a great player. Not like Richards, who was so obviously brilliant from the word go. Chappell developed season by season and he's still maturing. I doubt if we'll know how good he is for another two years. Even now any Test side welcomes the sight of Greg Chappell's backside disappearing into the pavilion. I make no secret of the fact I was delighted he failed so often in England. But I was nevertheless very worried because he was overdue for a big score, and for someone who can play shots all round the wicket, tension builds up when he walks to the crease.

I can only hope, for cricket's sake, that the captaincy doesn't affect Chappell's natural brilliance, for we haven't seen the best of Greg Chappell yet.

So there are my top six, all with their own particular brand of play, but all great batsmen.

There are so many others close to the top bracket, who certainly deserve a mention. Ian Chappell and Rohan Kanhai immediately come to mind.

Chappell's renowned as a fighter. He doesn't play according to the coaching manual, yet he's rated by team-mates as the best batsman Australia has on all wickets and against all attacks. I'm not in the position to agree or disagree with that statement. I can only rate him as I've found him in opposition.

Ross Edwards. *I keep an eye on another Edwards cover drive*

David Steele *by name and nature with Deryck Murray looking on*

I love to drive: *Rod Marsh and Gary Gilmour watch the result*

Greg Chappell. *A cover drive for the textbook, Brisbane in 1975 against West Indies*

Sunil Gavaskar. *The little Indian can tear an attack apart, and his pants*

Like his brother, I'm always delighted to see him out of the way, and his record for Australia does give substance to his standing among Australians. He can drive and pull after shuffling into line, but his hook shot is always uppish and a potential danger to himself, though he's got a lot of runs from it.

To me he's always a big candidate for a leg-before-wicket decision because he shuffles across the crease. That's always dangerous, especially in England, where the ball is more inclined to move around off the seam. But Chappell plays the ball very late and that is what saves him. It is always a sign of a fine player.

Kanhai is different from most West Indian batsman, but then that can be attributed to many years of County cricket. He's more the coaching-manual-type batsman, right down to rolling his hands over when hooking, quickly getting the ball onto the turf. But he has many extra shots of his own, all just as effective.

In a crisis Kanhai can switch to the dour role, as he proved in the Prudential World Cup final against Australia when he willingly played second fiddle to a rampaging Lloyd and certainly made it easier for him. Had Kanhai fallen early, I doubt if Lloyd could have found a partner willing to get down the other end the way Kanhai did.

There are a host of others who, on their day, or even in one particular series, have shown enough to make one speculate that they could kick on to greatness. For England, Dennis Amiss went within three runs of breaking Bobby Simpson's world record of 1,393 runs in a calendar year and that's a great feat. I might add that I have seen few batsmen perform the way he did that tour. Amiss went through horrors against his bogeyman Dennis Lillee, and has therefore not kicked ahead again, though he will.

Pakistan's Majid Khan and Mushtaq Mohammad have had their moments of glory. Majid can be and has been a world-beater, but he seems to lack something at times and as a result has not consistently turned in the same performances. Mushtaq is a little impetuous, but once he gets in the groove he's one of the hardest men to get out. out.

In the large-as-life West Indies Alvin Kallicharran and Lawrence Rowe could well jump into the top bracket within five years. Kallicharran is a young, exciting left-hander of the Sobers mould, ever so keen to get on with it. Rowe was the first to start his Test career with a double and single century. That was against New Zealand. Then he peeled off a triple hundred against us, so all the ingredients are there for a great player. He's a far steadier batsman than most of his team-mates, so there's less chance of something going amiss.

Sunny Gavaskar is the only other batsman apart from Rowe and Doug Walters to score a double and single century in the same Test, that was against West Indies in the Caribbean. Gavaskar can be a West Indian type batsman, like Kallicharran he is very small in stature and therefore at a disadvantage against truly quick bowling on receptive wickets. He is versatile and can play the 'shut up shop' role.

Where I can play shots just above my waist, Kallicharran and Gavaskar are struggling to get out of the way although both love to hook.

Ian Redpath, *steadying influence*

In Australia there have been many who served their country with distinction. Walters is a devastating player on his day, Keith Stackpole could cut and hook savagely and was a tough competitor. I had many a run in with Stacky, but admired him as a player. Ian Redpath has been a steadying influence, both as an opening batsman and in the middle order where he prefers to bat.

New Zealand's Glenn Turner has made himself into a solid, no-risk type player. Opening the batting for his country places tremendous pressure on the right-hander. Early in his career he hardly had the strength to hit the ball off the square, but he's a different proposition now.

Then you have crisis players like Basil d'Oliveira, Ray Illingworth and Alan Knott for England; Ross Edwards and Rod Marsh for Australia and Bevan Congdon for New Zealand. They have the temperament to dig in, stop the rot and in many cases score runs as well.

But the man on the fringe I admire possibly more than any others is the Nawab of Pataudi. Having lost his eye in a car accident, Tiger Pataudi fought back to be still a top-class Test batsman.

Despite his affliction, he retained a sharp sense of humour. Admittedly I've heard this story second-hand, for I wasn't around when it happened, but it typified Tiger's love of the practical joke. It was a good few years ago, at a time when Nawabs in India were all-powerful. England was in India and between games Tiger invited half a dozen of the tourists to a tiger hunt. He warned them all that there had been some trouble recently with the odd bandit or two, but as he was so well respected

and would be with them, there was no danger. Out they went and just after dark, towards the end of a most exciting day, the party was ambushed. The Englishmen went white with fear, but Tiger told them not to worry, everything would be straightened out.

While the entire party was held at gun point against their vehicles, with the raiders' car lights right on them, Tiger strode over to the leader telling him that his guests were English Test cricketers and to let them go unharmed. The leader took no notice, raised his rifle and fired point-blank into Tiger's chest.

Tiger crumpled, clutching his heart as blood poured everywhere. If the cricketers were white before, they went colourless at that stage. Here they were in the middle of nowhere, with their insurance policy, the Nawab of Pataudi, dead as a doornail on the ground. Suddenly Tiger jumped up hysterical with laughter. He'd organised the whole thing with his boys. The shot was a blank, the blood a sac of animal's blood that he'd squashed against his chest. From the cricketer's point of view, they were too shattered to see the funny side.

Pataudi was like that. He couldn't let a chance slip by to crack a joke, or play a practical joke. And he could really bat, just a fraction short of being classed among the greats. It wasn't easy having to play so well so often in a side that wasn't rated in those days.

So there are the men who have conquered the ball—batsmen of all shapes, sizes and ability with one thing in common, their ability to score runs in all conditions.

The Finger Men

The Great Spinners

The art of spin—guile and patience, yet frustration, That's the unhappy lot of present-day spinners, making the best in my time something right out of the box. It's a lot more difficult to be a top-class spinner now than it was, say 10 years ago, and long before that. Certainly this applies in England where so many one-day games are played. It's part and parcel of seven-day-a-week cricket, making it mighty tough on any up-and-coming youngster who wants to be a spinner.

My top finger men all learned their trade—and it's the most demanding of the lot—long before the advent of the one-day game. Demanding it is and the frustrations can be crucifying. Imagine leaving out the likes of Lance Gibbs, Srinivas Venkataraghavan, Erapalli Prasanna, Chandrasekhar, Ashley Mallett and the magnificent Bishen Bedi from such a superb and highly-contested competition as the Prudential World Cup.

It's unbelievable. They are all world-rated spinners, yet the accepted way to play this type of game doesn't lend itself to playing them, as so many think. For my part I'd have all of them in their respective sides, purely because they are great masters of their art.

But it appears it's to be a seamer's game, a game of cat and mouse where batsmen are contained and as a result of frustration they succumb. But there's always room for a class spinner, no matter what the competition. They take time to reach cricketing maturity, but once they are there, their presence is not only priceless, it can turn a game in a matter of overs.

One-day cricket takes the spinners out of their groove, more's the pity. Off-spinners become flat to economise and leg spinners are scarce as hen's teeth. Having passed their apprenticeship with flying colours, my top finger men have to take a back seat when limited-over cricket takes over.

There are no finer spinners than the Indians, born and bred on wickets that certainly don't suit pacemen. It's far too hot to churn out a lot of overs with pace and the Indians aren't so strong and sturdy as their counterparts in other countries. The wickets also combine to ensure that country's standing as a spinner's domain, rather than the home of an all-round pace attack.

It's true that up in the north there are any number of big men who spend their sporting time excelling at hockey. There have been moves afoot to entice these giants into cricket, but so far to no avail. Out of my top six, three are Indians—Bishen Bedi, Chandrasekhar and Prasanna, what a trio. The last time we were in India I saw Bedi and Chandra bowl unbelievably well—my words cannot describe how brilliant they were—for five Test matches.

That was nearly three years ago, and it could also be said that I saw them at their best, although I can't agree that Bedi had a season out of this world for he's an out-of-this-world bowler ninety per cent of the time. So turbaned Sikh Bishen Bedi tops my list.

A colourful character, Bishen is also a true sportsman who can applaud a good shot, even off his own bowling. He's a fine bloke, a tough competitor in his own quiet way and a great spinner. Add all that to his smooth approach and free-flowing left arm action and there's little wonder that with his seemingly unbendable temperament Bedi is a world-beater. Bedi has the classical loop and he

Bishen Bedi. *The classical Indian is my top finger man*

Intikhab Alam, *currently the best leg spinner in the world*

gives the ball a real rip, he has a quicker ball, a drifter, a big spin ball, and an arm ball. Bishen Bedi has the lot, he can bowl you four different deliveries right on the spot every over.

Bedi's temperament adds the caviar. You never really know if you're getting on top, because he's just as likely to mess you up at a time when you think you're sitting pretty. If Bedi sees you hitting in an area where he believes you're playing with fire, he'll let you go, knowing he'll eventually get you.

Like Chandra and Prasanna, Bedi has been blessed with tremendous support from close-to-the-wicket fielders in Venkat and Eknath Solkar. That's a priceless asset close to the bat and around the corner. I've often been asked whether Bedi is a better bowler in India than anywhere else in the world. I've always answered that it doesn't matter—Bedi can bowl brilliantly anywhere, and at any time. He's at his best when the breeze comes in from the third man area, allowing his left-armers to drift in. From there Bedi can either straighten the ball up, or let it carry on towards the legside cordon.

I have never seen Bedi let a side down. Sure he's bowled some bad spells, anyone can do that, but overall he's great value. During that last tour in India, Bedi came on first change with the shine very much evident. He followed Solkar to the bowling crease. Classic fieldsman that he is, Solkar went into the record books as the only new ball bowler to go through an entire series without taking a wicket. It mattered not, his sole task was to take just a nick or two out of the ball and let Bedi take over for over after over. I can't praise Bishen Bedi enough, he's a marvellous bowler and a marvellous character.

In Melbourne during the World XI tour in 1971–72 we were thumped by Australia in a one-day so badly that another smaller version was put on for the large crowd, to fill in the time left. I had been only too happy to help Bish with his yards and yards of silk that made up his many turbans. I still believe it was Bedi who sowed the seed in Sobers' mind for an antic that made the crowd crazy with delight.

When he was just about ready to take the field, Sobers said 'Greigy, if you wear a turban onto the field, you can lead us out'. I thought to myself 'That can't be bad', and it wasn't. To the roar of the spectators out came a six-foot-seven South African-born English cricketer to open the bowling dressed up to the nines in a brilliantly coloured turban. For me, that's where the fun finished, even though it had been a big thing in my cricketing career.

After about five balls I thought my neck was broken, the thing was so heavy. All the joy of leading out the World side went by the boards in a hurry. To have my all-time hero Garry Sobers coming out behind me was certainly a thrill, remembering I hadn't played a Test to that stage.

I didn't want to hurt Bishen's feelings, but I just had to admit that the damn thing was painful. To which Bish replied, 'You might be a big man Greigy, but only the strongest can wear the turban'. I couldn't argue with that, not at any price.

Heaven only knows how much those turbans cost. I well remember standing some fifteen yards away from Bedi in the dressing room holding one end as he twined it around his arm like rope. From there he very carefully wound the magnificent silk around the underhat until it became a work of art. That's

Freddie Titmus, *lost four toes, but never his ability*

Two in two and Derek Underwood claims the wickets of Rod Marsh and John Inverarity in successive balls to win the Headingley Test in 1972, taking 6–45 in the second innings

Mushtaq Mohammad, *leg spinners to support his batting*

a lot of cloth, but then Bishen Bedi's a lot of cricketer and the crowds love him.

But despite Bedi's brilliance, I have no hesitation in saying that Chandra's bowling in that series in India was the best I've ever seen. We had been told that patience would net at least two balls an over that could be smashed for four, but watch out for the others. By the time the fourth Test came around and still no loose ball, we had to admit that Chandra was something special. I'd heard lots of stories about him, funny action but different, attacking but inaccurate. Was that theory blasted!

Chandra's repertoire was immense, his only shortcoming lack of physical strength. He played only in the Test matches, then had to rest. I think I'm right in saying that as a kid he had polio, resulting in a withered arm. So I had tremendous admiration for his grit and determination, but add that to his normal googly, his leg spinner that was rare but dangerous, his fizz ball—a bouncing wrong 'un that hit the deck and took off—and his incredibly quick faster ball. That all totalled trouble, especially the fizz ball that caused so much strife in the short leg position.

I well remember Keith Fletcher's off stump careering out of the slot and almost spearing keeper Farokh Engineer en route. It landed some five yards back with Fletch looking on in disbelief. There hadn't been any change in delivery, but the net result was devastating, proof enough of Chandra's faster ball.

So that was Chandra's series. He hasn't bowled as well before or since, but in those five Tests he was magic. It's just a shame he's so inconsistent, but he'll always be uppermost in my memory. Anyone who can bowl so well

in the most difficult of all spin, fast to very fast leg spin, deserves all possible praise.

That brings me to Prasanna, and it will never cease to amaze me how many times he's been dropped from the Test side. Admittedly Bedi and Chandra, along with Venkat, make it very hard for selectors to find another spin spot, but Prasanna is a world-class off-spinner worthy of his place in any country's lineup. I place him in the same category as England's Freddie Titmus, they are like two peas in a pod. Both have the classical loop. They spin the ball or through sheer control allow it to carry on through, and like all their ilk they look for the inconsistent bounce. Therefore they have the extra bow to their armoury as compared with the other class spinners like Lance Gibbs, Venkat, Ashley Mallett, Derek Underwood and Ray Illingworth. They all bowl in a flat trajectory, cutting down their effectiveness. As for Prasanna and Chandra, I couldn't believe it when they were left out of the Prudential World Cup squad. To me, Bedi, Chandra and Prasanna should have been first picked. And to top it all off, Bedi was left out of the first game against England. That decision was incredible.

Prasanna has always worried me, Titmus the same. In fact they are Bishen Bedi the other way round. It's almost impossible to pick their off-spinner from the out-swinger, and obviously there's a lot of difference if you make a mistake, more than likely it's history.

You might hit Prasanna or Titmus through extra cover for four on the front foot, but you always have that feeling that they're conning you, they've got something up their sleeves. You wonder whether or not next time there's

Clive Lloyd, *always on hand, just fails to run out*
Notts' Mike Smedley and Alvin Kallicharran joins
in the appeal

Greg Chappell, ever so strong on the leg side, too strong for Bob Woolmer to cut off runs at Lord's

Below

Close, and I manage to get out of harm's way as Bevan Congdon moves into a cover drive

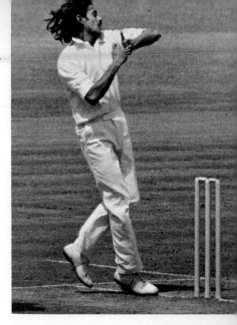

Srinivas Venkataraghavan, *a flat, but very successful spinner*

going to be a little extra tweek on the ball that will find the gate between bat and pad, or it's going to hurry through for the same result. You can never be certain. The ball's in the same place, but it does something different and you're gone.

Titmus and Prasanna are the two best off-spinners I've ever played against. To me they are the classic off-spinners. They have such superb variation because of the pace they bowl, and they have great control. They flight the ball, spin it, drift it, they go through the whole card. What more can you say about them, their records speak for themselves.

As for Titmus, his comeback was as classical as his action. During the tour of the West Indies in 1967 Titmus was frollicking alongside a boat that had its propeller in the middle, rather than at the back. Freddie felt something in the water, saw some blood and was pulled aboard.

He didn't think anything about it as team-mates frantically wrapped a towel around his foot and carted him off to hospital. They were very upset, especially Colin Cowdrey. They all knew it was very serious, but said nothing. A Canadian specialist was found and all Freddie did was to look at the doctor's face. Little Fred never did like the sight of blood, especially his own. When the expression on the doctor's face failed to change as he took off the blood-soaked towel, Fred was very relieved. He felt no pain, and wasn't even worried when he was wheeled into the operating theatre. Once out of the anaesthetic, Freddie was told that he'd lost all four toes and only had the big one left.

It was then that Fred reckoned it started to hurt, and how. Titmus came home, and it took a lot of adjustment to try to regain his delicate bowling balance on the one big toe, even though it's the most important of the lot. But regain it he did, and today he's still one of the world's great off-spinners, despite being on the wrong side of forty.

Enter Lancelot Gibbs, one of the all-time greats in this department. The tall, spindly West Indian has bowled more overs than anyone else I'm going to talk about. Keith Miller, that magnificent post-war Aussie all-rounder, summed it up best in a report that was read world wide. He had just seen Lance bowl his ten-thousandth ball in Test cricket. Said Miller, 'That's a lot of balls'. Apt, and to the point. Now Gibbs has passed the 25,000 mark, and at the time of writing he is within spitting distance of Freddie Trueman's world record of 307 Test wickets. No doubt he'll pass the mighty total, a credit to a very dedicated cricketer who's been on the scene for over two decades.

Gibbs falls in a bracket somewhere in between the loop of Titmus and Prasanna and the flatter off-spinners like Mallett and Illingworth. His greatest asset is bounce—everything about Lance Gibbs is just that. He bounces into the wicket, he bounces around the field and rightfully gives the impression he loves every minute of the game. But he can be frustrated quite easily. Lance's whole approach is to bowl maidens, sixty-second maidens if possible. He works on the theory that he'll bowl thirty-plus overs an innings, and therefore has time to wear a batsman out, snap his patience, then send him on his way.

Gibbs bounces back to his mark, wheels on the point of his toe and bounces in. Rarely does he look at the batsman, so I've found it

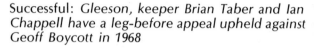

Successful: *Gleeson, keeper Brian Taber and Ian Chappell have a leg-before appeal upheld against Geoff Boycott in 1968*

helpful to drop my eyes towards my bat, forcing him to stop his approach midstream. Lance doesn't take too kindly to that, and it can upset his rhythm. But as that's the only dentable part of Lance Sibb's makeup, it's easy to see why he's such a class bowler.

After bowling so many deliveries Gibbs has a huge callous on the index finger of his right hand. It's so bad, it's almost grotesque. He can actually move it around from the inside of the finger to the other side. Yet it doesn't stop him being naggingly accurate and the mere fact he's lasted so long is a credit to his endurance. Gibbs hasn't the same full repertoire as Titmus or Prasanna, but his magic has meant a lot to the West Indies on wickets that in the main have not been conducive to his art.

The only loopy leg spinner I rate in the top bracket is Pakistan's Test captain Intikhab Alam. Inti has been shuffled around by the Pakistan Board as captain, but he's shuffled many a top-rated batsman out with his variation and attacking cricket. Intikhab is a good thinker with the ball. The same can't be said of his batting, even though he's one of the hardest hitters in the game.

Leg spinning seems to be a dying art. With Robin Hobbs retired from the County scene, there isn't another English leg spinner in the country. Intikhab, with Surrey, and Pakistan Test team-mate Mushtaq Mohammad, with Northants, are the only leg spinners left, and that's a crying shame. Out of all the bowling arts leg spinning is the hardest to conquer. After all, the ball must come out of the back of the hand, increasing the element of risk.

Any leg spinner worth his salt must have a big heart, and Inti's got that, and more. There

are few more likeable fellows in international cricket. Though Inti's had more to sour him off than most, rarely does that jovial grin leave his face.

Despite his solid physique, Inti is very quick on his feet. During the World XI tour of Australia he challenged Farokh Engineer, India's Test keeper on that tour, to a match race over about 100 yards. This side had every big cricket country represented, England, South Africa, India, Pakistan, West Indies and New Zealand, and when the bets were placed out came pounds, rupees, dollars, rand, the lot. The race took place in Tasmania with a highly confident Farokh keen to clean up. After a false start or two, Farokh shot away from the blocks, with a hint of beating the gun. In the first fifteen yards Inti was trailing badly some three behind. By the halfway stage Inti was further behind, then his momentum took over. Bit by bit Inti bridged the gap to finally roll onto victory, leaving a very disconsolate Farokh panting hard. That's a fair indication as to Inti's fighting heart.

I don't know what would have happened had Inti not shown such strength on that tour. He held it all together so often with Sobers on the injured list and under heavy fire from the Press about his time spent on the golf course.

Inti carefully and feelingly kept so many possible factions from coming to grips. When war broke out between India and Pakistan while we were in Perth, it was Inti's leadership qualities that again came to the fore. There were three Pakistanis, Inti, Zaheer Abbas and Asif Masood; and three Indians, Farokh, Sunny Gavaskar and Bishen Bedi. It could have been ugly, but thanks to Inti all went well. So Inti is quite a guy.

Ray Illingworth, *always tight, and a hard man to get away*

Next page

Lance Gibbs, *all concentration, poise and perfect balance*

Gibbs again. *He jubilantly throws the ball high after victim Geoff Boycott was caught and bowled at The Oval in 1973. Keeper Deryck Murray and captain Rohan Kanhai look on*

His leg-spinning repertoire includes all the accepted deliveries, and then some. His normal leg spinner drifts in towards the batsman, he bowls a good googly, and a disguised one giving him an extra string to his bow, a quicker round-armer as a surprise, and a flipper that has toppled all the best players.

So these are my top six finger men. Although there are others who have proved themselves in top company, they come into a second category behind Bedi, Chandra, Prasanna, Gibbs, Titmus and Intikhab. But let me make it quite clear that everyone I'm about to talk about now rates very highly. They are Derek Underwood, Ray Illingworth, Venkat, Ashley Mallett, Mushtaq Moham-mad, Hedley Howarth, Terry Jenner and Johnny Gleeson.

'Deadly' Derek isn't in the classic mould of a spinner, but on receptive wickets there's no better finger man in the world.

Illingworth slots into the Titmus-Prasanna mould, but there are no frills about his bowling. He never experiments and plugs away waiting patiently for a batsman to become impatient. And it works.

Illingworth is the perfect example of how the game's played now, against, say, ten years ago. It's a cat-and-mouse game. In the days gone by every bowler set out to take a wicket every ball. Nowadays it's very different, it's more containment than attack, and I think that's a pity. I'm all for attack at every opportunity, but the one-day games have certainly made a big change in everyday thinking. That's why containing cricketers like Illingworth have taken over, far more than ever before. But let me say

that Ray Illingworth was the best captain I've played under, and I'll say more about that later. For now, I don't believe Illingworth ever used himself enough and if he was playing under me I would certainly have used him more.

Mallett and Venkat go together, although Mallett has been far more successful. But, like Illingworth, they are flat off-spinners with their own individual variations.

Mallett is a fine bowler, with a great record to prove it. It would be interesting to know what would have happened to his career if he had spent more time in England. Unfortu-nately, the tall Australian was the victim of Australian conditions that don't allow more than five on the on side. In England, where we can have six, Mallett would have been able to move away from a straight off-stump type of line and bowl more at the wicket.

His high action ensures bounce, something that Titmus and Prasanna can't get. That's what makes him such a good bowler, but more time in England could have seen him even better. Off-spinners aren't rated in Australia, yet Mallett's hundredth Test wicket came up in twenty-three Tests as compared with Dennis Lillee's twenty-two. That's a statistic that will make a few blink.

Mallett's flat trajectory would have been changed in England, giving him an extra drop on the batsmen. He would have developed a loop or arc in delivery and bowled more around the wicket. It happened to Gibbs. It took Warwickshire two seasons to get Lance to bowl around the wicket on slow turners where the ball almost stopped. But nothing can be taken away from Ashley Mallett. He's

bowled magnificently for Australia where there were more wickets working against him than for him.

Venkat hasn't been as successful as Mallett, but he is very much the same type of off-spinner. In India, where the wickets are helpful, Venkat can be unplayable. Although a fine bowler, he's been inconsistent overall.

Confusion was Johnny Gleeson's claim to fame. He slotted the ball in front of his middle finger, and flicked it out like an orange pip. Many of the world's best batsmen struggled to pick him up. I found it easier to pick the ball spinning in the air rather than trying to work it out from his fingers, because that's where all the confusion comes from.

Gleeson was at his best in South Africa, where there are very few spinners and he created real havoc there. He was an unlucky bowler. Countless times he beat the bat, yet failed to get an edge. And he wasn't blessed with great close fielding support as were Bedi, Prasanna and Chandra. Many a catch went begging, but Gleeson was a tough competitor who kept plugging away. He is a great team man.

Hedley Howarth deserves special mention. In a basically weak side, it says volumes for his left-arm spinners that he's New Zealand's strike bowler. He's got the lot, flight, drift and spin, and even though he's not on the same level as Bedi, Howarth would make most Test sides around the world, for he's a class bowler.

Here I've talked basically about finger spinners, for wrist spinners are at such a premium there aren't many of international standard about. Australia's Terry Jenner and Pakistan's Mushtaq Mohammad rate highly.

Jenner is the best leg spinner in Australia, but has at times been treated badly. It's beyond me how Jenner could have been picked in all six Tests against us in Australia, yet missed out on the tour to England. And he's consistently been picked in the 12 for years, only to find himself carrying the drinks. His only major tour was to the West Indies, and he certainly proved his worth there. Like Mallett, he suffers from the anti-spin movement in Australia, though both are world-class spinners.

Mushtaq has his batting to look to, but thoroughly enjoys leg spinning as a supporting role. He's far better than average, but I don't rate him anywhere near Intikhab as a leggie though there have been times when Mushtaq has caused plenty of bother with the ball.

Life is hard for leg spinners. By their very nature they have to be attacking bowlers, buying wickets and enticing batsmen to have a crack at them. But, as I said before, these days containment is the name of the game. A leg spinner has to get plenty of work. Under the present set up where's a young leg spinner going to get the experience to make the top? Leg spinners could die out in the next decade, for although finger spinners are playing a bigger role every season the proof of the leg spinner's plight is underlined in the fact that only Inti, Jenner, Mushtaq and Chandra even rate a mention in this chapter. The rest are all finger spinners, but I hope it doesn't rest there for the future. That would be a sad indictment of the game.

The Work-Horses
The Medium-Pacers

Work horses churn out a lot of overs and incur the wrath of spectators who often believe they make the game boring. They are nevertheless a vital part of any team's attack, though they rarely get credit for the job they do. Over a five-day Test there have got to be stages where the batsmen have to be contained, where someone will have to pin an end down for long periods. More importantly, it must be done cheaply.

Every country must have at least one work horse, while some are fortunate to have more. Two that readily come to mind are Max Walker of Australia and Derek Underwood of England. Walker has been the poor relation to the Thomson-Lillee combination, but neither would have been so successful if Walker hadn't done his thankless job so well.

Walker has made it possible for Thomson and Lillee to rest. He invariably has to bowl uphill into the wind for a huge number of overs, leaving strikers like Thomson and Lillee to fire away downhill with the wind. Obviously the main requirement for a work horse is accuracy, pin-point accuracy in both line and length. Walker has this to perfection. Despite an awkward approach and windmill delivery that hardly give the impression of a great bowler, there's no doubt about it that he genuinely is.

He could never be spoken of as a blitzman, yet in his own field they don't come any better. Yet, given the chance, Walker can be a strike bowler. When Lillee broke down in the West Indies it was Walker who stepped into the breach with such success that he broke the record set by Neil Hawke for wickets taken in a series in the West Indies. He has proved he's versatile, and a mighty handy man to have in any side. If he was playing for England at the moment he would be a strike bowler. Obviously, in Australia, with Thomson and Lillee blazing away with full fury, his role is seemingly minor, but it's true proportions are far greater in the work-horse area.

Everything about Walker is ungainly. He walks very erect for a tall man, but he even looks uncomfortable doing that. He slides into the wicket, takes one big hop just prior to delivery and with a flurry of arms and legs, sends out his naggingly accurate medium pacers.

Underwood is vastly different in every way. As a left-armer who is neither a paceman nor a spinner in the true sense of the word, Underwood is smooth in everything he does. But, like Walker, he is flexible enough to be a striker or a work horse, each with a devastating effect. On a treacherous wicket Underwood becomes the deadliest spinner in the world, and I really mean deadly. The Australians found that out at Headingley in 1972 where Underwood ripped them apart and he's done that all over the world. On those days he's unplayable, but in good batting conditions Underwood is expected to return figures like 30 overs 1-30. He's hard to get away because for a spinner he's relatively swift through the air.

Underwood's flat trajectory stops a batsman rushing down the wicket to smash him over the top, yet he maintains such a tight line and length that more often than not it's a matter of waiting him out or taking a risk. Underwood's done a great job for England, as Ray Illingworth did in the same role.

So Walker and Underwood get my vote as the world's top work horses. But there are

Max Walker has made it all possible for Thomson and Lillee, here bowling to David Steele at Headingley in 1975

Bevan Congdon *has the full range as New Zealand's workhorse*

Lance Gibbs *is poetry in motion as he intently watches the flight of the ball*

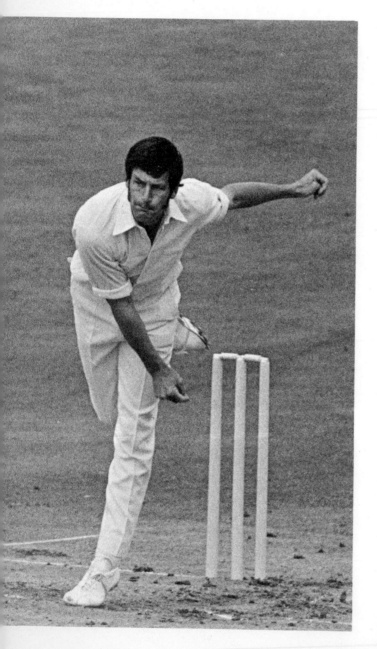

many others who have filled this role with distinction. One of the best examples has been Bevan Congdon. Unhappily for New Zealand there have been plenty of times when containment was the order of the day, and it's been Congdon who has churned out many an over of tight medium pace. He's probably the slowest of the medium-pace brigade, but he has many types of delivery to offset the possibility of being heavily punished.

Congdon can cut and move the ball both ways, has a good slower and faster ball and bowls well within himself. The Congdons of this world have the happy knack of picking up a wicket even though they don't look as if they are going to do so. Many a top batsman has said to himself, 'I fancy this sort of stuff', only to find that he has chopped a ball back onto the stumps or lofted one gently into the covers. All this goes for Australia's Doug Walters too. Walters is a renowned partnership breaker, doing just a little either way.

Rarely are work horses thrashed. If they are, the side is generally in terrible strife, chasing leather from one end of the field to the other.

In the West Indies, now that Andy Roberts has asserted himself, Keith Boyce knows only one way to bowl and that's screaming full bore, while young Michael Holding is starting to show all the signs of being a class speedster.

Strongman Vanburn Holder does a good job in a containment role. He can bowl for very long spells, takes a long run that is smooth to match his delivery, and is generally the ideal type of work horse for the excitable West Indians.

Lance Gibbs does virtually the same thing, but because he's so tight, Gibbs contains and

Terry Jenner, *in and out of the Aussie side, but keeps bouncing back*

Below
Bishen Bedi, *colourful turbans, carefully controlled left-arm spinners*

Opposite page
Ashley Mallett *watched by the huge Melbourne crowd*

Overleaf
Phil Edmonds, *England's Zambian-born left-arm spinner bowling to Australia's Rick McCosker. Umpire is Dickie Bird*

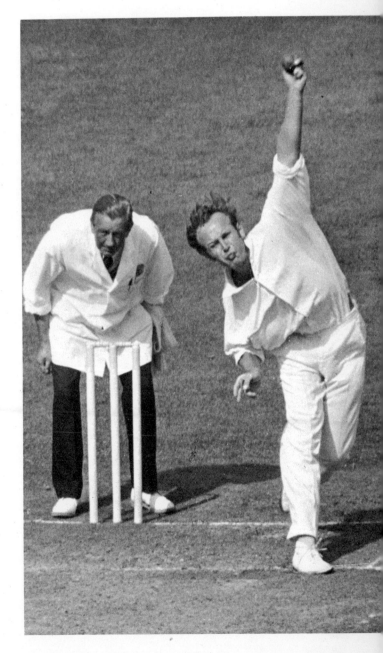

Derek Underwood, *so versatile he can be a strike bowler or a workhorse*

strikes. Like Underwood, he immediately becomes a striker when the conditions are right.

Little Abid Ali is India's opening bowler, but with the spinners as strikers he fills this hard role. Bedi does both, but Abid Ali, despite a massively long run that certainly isn't in keeping with his medium pace, has bowled many overs for few runs while the spinners have attacked from the other end.

Asif Iqbal is Pakistan's work horse. A little faster through the air than Congdon, Asif is an extremely fit cricketer who loves nothing better than being in the action.

If South Africa was playing Test cricket now Eddie Barlow would be the man. In the past he was just that and was fortunate to have Trevor Goddard and Tiger Lance in support. But in my time South Africa have won their games so easily that work horses weren't required. Everyone who picked up a ball got wickets, but of course that's the exception to the rule.

So for me work horses make strikers possible. Obviously, they only come into play when the strikers have failed, but the breathing space they give as they nag away allows the strikers to regather to fight another day. This is the sort of role I love to play. I could never be classed a strike bowler, even though I had to try to be just that during the World XI tour to Australia. But I'm not fast enough and never could be. Nevertheless, being able to switch from medium pace to off-spin keeps me in the game a lot more.

When we went to the West Indies in 1973 those blokes were in a murderous batting mood on good batting wickets. As a utility man I had to work out some method to keep

Abid Ali *has a hard role to fill for India, watched by
their ace left-armer Bishen Bedi*

Michael Holding *has just emerged as another West
Indian giant. Time will tell if he makes his mark
permanently*

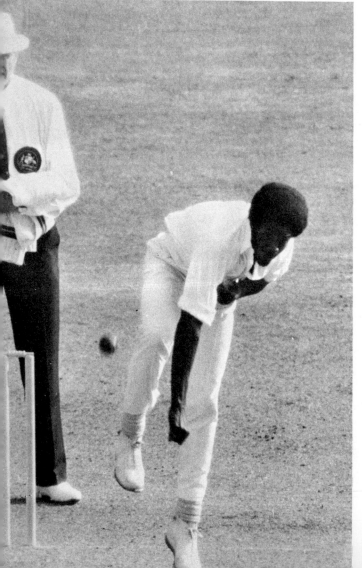

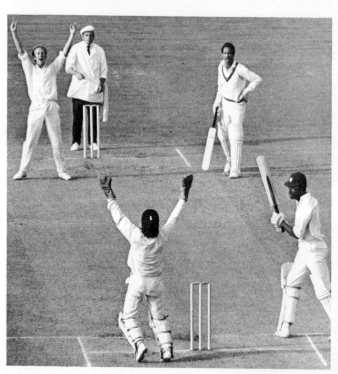

Success. *Umpire Dickie Bird about to give Clive
Lloyd out, caught behind by Alan Knott off
Underwood at Edgbaston in 1973, Garry Sobers
watching*

Exit Julien. *An excited Walker bowls Bernard Julien at Melbourne in 1975, watched by Clive Lloyd and Rod Marsh keeping*

Asif Iqbal, *extremely fit and revels in the action*

them quiet and trying to keep Clive Lloyd and company from blazing away wasn't easy. All I was armed with was a tattered and torn ball for most of the time, and that was like money for old rope for those fellows. It was just a matter of front foot down the wicket and smash. I got desperate, for my only hope was that they'd hit the ball straight to fielders and that didn't happen often enough. So I started to bowl off-spinners around the wicket, searching for the rough outside the off-stump. Because I used the same approach as my seamers, I could slip a few in here and there for variation. And it worked.

There were so many left-handers in the side, most of whom didn't like to be contained for long, that it wasn't hard to reason why it was so successful. In effect I was both striker and work horse. When Lawrence Rowe scored his 302 against us at Bridgetown, I started to think that if the wicket did turn, I'd be in business. That's exactly what happened. I got six wickets there, and finished with thirteen wickets in the last Test at Port of Spain, Trinidad, where we won to square the series. That gave me a lot of pleasure, because I'd worked on an idea and it paid off handsomely. Had I stuck to medium pacers I would have been thrashed.

With that personal experience, I can't praise the work horses enough. As a captain, I look to them to tidy up a game that's slipping away. And, as you will have noticed, most of the work horses I've mentioned have been all-rounders. In the main that's their role. It's only Walker, Underwood and Holder who are purely bowlers. So to this brand of cricketer I touch my cap. It's hard to realise their worth until you need them and then they're priceless.

7

The Jacks of All Trades

The All-Rounders

A perfect team would be five of the best batsmen in the world, a keeper who can bat, and five strike bowlers who are also the best in the business. Two of those five must be fine all-rounders to give the side depth. Obviously that's a dream.

So an all-rounder, the jack-of-all-trades, is vital to the success of any side. The more the merrier, for any side that is classed as great has quite a few all-rounders. It could be said that this is the hallmark of almost every successful team. There must be depth in batting and bowling to get into the great team category, you only have to look at the best teams in the world right now in Australia and the West Indies to see the proof.

Australia has strike men in Lillee and Thomson, a work horse in Walker and class spinners in Mallett and Jenner, plus the likes of Gilmour, the Chappells, and Walters. That's true depth, because Lillee, Thomson, Walker, Gilmour, Mallett and Jenner have all scored sound runs and Walters and the Chappells have taken vital wickets.

The West Indies are probably even better off in this regard. Keith Boyce, Bernard Julien and now young Michael Holding bat right down the list, but are just as capable of scoring a Test fifty as many other batsmen who bat higher up the list in other countries. That's a delightful position to be in, and just goes to show how important it is to have all-rounders, two players in one if you like, so that in fact there are about fifteen players in the team.

I recognise five of the best. The doyen of them all is Garry Sobers, then come Mike Procter, Eddie Barlow, Basil d'Oliveira and Ray Illingworth. Sobers is king. There hasn't been anyone like him before, and I'm quite convinced there'll never be anyone better than him in the future. Not only was he one of the greatest batsmen the world's ever seen, but he could bowl as fast as Wes Hall or Charlie Griffith when he put his mind to it, switch to left-arm orthodox spin, or even chinamen and googlies, field in any position absolutely brilliantly, throw with either hand and keep as well as most.

There's nobody, just nobody, as accomplished as that. There are those that say that if Garry had one failing, it was his captaincy. They've often wondered why a player so fantastic in everything he did could be a 'bad' captain? For openers, I don't believe he was a 'bad' captain. I believe Garfield Sobers was categorised as a captain on the same level as a player and that's one hell of a standard to live up to. If he was going to be that good we might as well all have gone home when he was playing.

Captains are only as good as their players, yet Sobers was so great, it's reasonable to assume he could have led any side out of the woods on his own. Sobers as a captain wanted nothing more than a good, entertaining game. Naturally, he tried to provide it himself. For him, a boring game was like being locked up in the Tower of London with the key thrown away. He's been roundly criticised over the years, especially in the West Indies, for losing Test matches with a declaration. But that's the man, and one of the many reasons why I admire him so much.

Sober's versatility is beyond comprehension. Already I've mentioned him as one of the great batsmen and bowlers, and I'll do the same again when we get to fieldsmen, what

Garry Sobers, the greatest all-rounder of them all

Illingworth cuts, *this time off New Zealand's Bevan Congdon at Headingley in 1973, watched by Ken Wadsworth*

more can the man do?

Just take his bowling—his batting is legendary. Here was a player who could bowl as fast as anyone has ever seen, move the ball extremely late in either direction, revert to world-class spinners in any fashion, and get rid of the best batsmen going around. Is it any wonder Garfield Sobers has been rated a one-man team? In one Test in the West Indies the selectors weren't too sure about Inshan Ali. Sobers hadn't been playing for a while, yet they picked him, and what did he do? He filled the role of medium-pacer, left-arm orthodox, left arm out-of-the-back-of-the-hand bowling Chinamen and googlies, which was thoroughly confusing.

When he came on you didn't just take up your stance and look around the field. You had first to establish what he was going to bowl. And if you didn't like facing left-arm spin or whatever, you'd be hoping and praying he hadn't worked it out. But that was wishful thinking, he knew and you copped what you didn't want. There'll never be another Sobers, that's for sure.

I'm eternally grateful to Sobers for, along with Sir Donald Bradman, he gave me my chance to get to the top with the World XI tour to Australia. When a host of talented all-rounders couldn't make that hastily put together trip, Sobers asked for me and Bradman went along with it purely because Sobers requested it. Sobers put me, a virtual unknown, on the road.

Sobers wanted the game to be alive, that's why he surrounded himself with the type of players who thought the same way. I'll always respect him for that. It mattered not that he played golf, that was his way of getting away

from it all. He loved it and played it well.

Towards the end of his great career, Sobers had trouble with his knees. Before that he could do anything, moving like a gazelle between wickets and in the field. Poetry in motion best described Sobers. Yet he was the best backward short-leg fieldsman I've ever seen, such was his unbelievable ability. It's the most difficult position to field in, but that's probably why Sobers was so good there. It was a challenge and for him there weren't many left—he'd conquered the majority. Sir Garfield Sobers is cricket's knight, he's tops in almost every department.

This is a challenge that Mike Procter faces now, possible the biggest challenge of his life. Knee trouble has forced Procter out of cricket for long periods in the last twelve months. The blitzman tag doesn't apply right now. Hopefully it will again, for Procter's and cricket's sake. But if it doesn't, Procter the batsman is going to have to find a hook shot.

For Mike Procter, extreme paceman, is on a promise from quite a few opponents he's faced over the years. Rarely has Procter ever faced a bouncer, for the bowler knew only too well that he'd cop one back, far faster, and far more lethal. If Procter's speed career is over, he's so versatile that I would almost bet he'll become a world-class spinner. Already he's taken seven wickets with his off-spinners, for Rhodesia in the Currie Cup, the side he captains. A 'wrong-footed' blitzman, Procter has a smooth delivery as an off-spinner. Admittedly, it's pretty hard to bowl offies off the wrong foot! Right now I wouldn't rate him, but he's like Titmus, giving the ball plenty of air, and he's a big spinner of the ball.

Derek Underwood *moves into his delivery stride.*
John Edrich in the background

Overleaf

Max Walker *off the ground as he bowls to Bernard*
Julien, Melbourne 1975, watched by umpire Robin
Bailhache

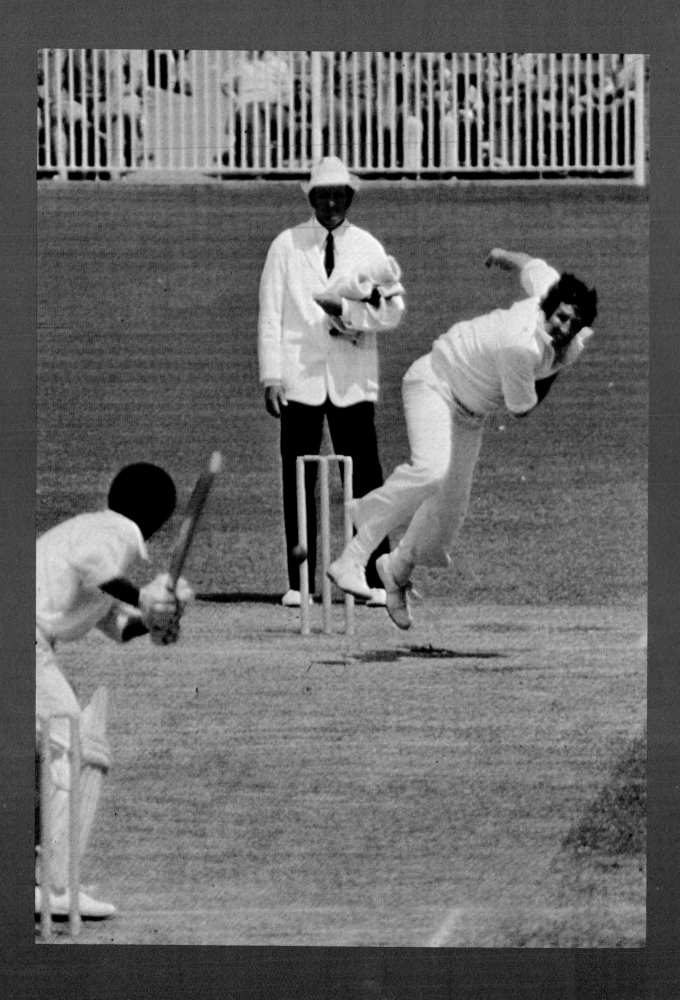

Keith Boyce *is at his best when he's aggressive with bat and ball*

Procter is the closest all-rounder to Garry Sobers. Fully fit he is mighty fast, a middle-order batsman capable of tearing any attack apart all round the wicket, and he is a brilliant fieldsman.

It's not often that a true paceman, someone as aggressively fast as Procter, also doubles up as an equally great batsman but Mike Procter is a complete cricketer. So too is South Africa's effervescent Eddie Barlow, a bubbling character who does not know the meaning of defeat. Barlow has yet to appear among the greats, but among the jacks-of-all-trades, only two come better.

The most striking thing about Barlow is that he believes so much in himself. I can remember the first time I was listening to the radio to hear South Africa playing Australia, with Trevor Goddard as captain. It was before my time, but I'd heard about this feeling that Barlow occasionally got—it would crop up every now and then in a match. Unless he was bowled right away, Barlow reckoned his chances of getting wickets were considerably lessened. And at that stage Barlow was in the side as a batsman and rarely ever used as a bowler. So when I heard that Barlow was frantically trying to attract Goddard's attention, I waited with some anticipation to see what the skipper would do.

The crowd at Castle Corner in Durban was doing everything in its power to assist Barlow, and eventually Goddard got the message and on came Barlow. He got three wickets in no time. From then on, whenever Barlow got that 'feeling', there was no doubt he'd get the ball. He's the most confident little bloke of all time. It's well known that Eddie Barlow could walk on water if he put his mind to it. To a

certain extent I have the same reputation in England and South Africa. It's not to be taken lightly, we are very alike in really believing in ourselves, that's what makes us tick.

I recall walking into the Newlands dressing room recently just after I'd signed up with St Peter, the international cricket gear manufacturer. I was carrying the pale blue bag with the large ST PETER embossed in black. Barlow's comment was true to form, 'We've always been competing with each other, but now that you've got St Peter on your side, I might be struggling'.

But what of Barlow the jack-of-all-trades? First, he's an opening batsman with a deceptive stance because he takes his guard at centre, then stands well outside the leg stump. From there he shuffles into line where he cuts and pulls so well. That's the way he started, keeping only to those two shots.

These days the industrious Barlow has geared himself for the whole range of shots. The Barlow nick over slips is legendary. Because Barlow is Barlow, he dogmatically states he means to play it. It's a controlled shot that nets him any number of runs. Many people have called it lucky, but he keeps on doing it so regularly that you begin to wonder and even agree with him.

As a slips fielder there are few better. He's not brilliant, but he makes few mistakes. No doubt, Barlow is a busybody. He runs all over the place, picks the ball up and throws well. He just can't keep still and he can't stop chattering. He's one of the most verbal players in slips anywhere in the world. But that's the guy, always on the move.

When he picks up the ball to bowl, that's where the real Edgar Barlow shines through.

Opposite page

Eddie Barlow, *a bubbling character who doesn't know the meaning of defeat*

Mike Procter, *the closest all rounder to the mighty Sobers*

Even if a batsman plays the ball in the middle of the bat straight down the wicket, Barlow's arms would be up in the air. For some incredible reason Barlow would ask, 'How in God's name did you middle that?'. To Barlow it's all part of the game. In one way he's stirring you up. In another he's lulling you into a sense of false security, making you wonder how did you middle that 'super ball'.

If a batsman plays and misses, Barlow is all over the place. But you don't have to miss the ball for Barlow to think he's bowled you an absolute jaffa. To him, every ball is a jaffa, to be treated with untold respect. Even if it's a full toss, to Barlow that's a surprise ball, one he had up his sleeve, and he'll go to great lengths after the game to tell you why. In the end you might even believe it, for Barlow's a very convincing fellow. He just exudes confidence.

As captain he leads from the front. In many ways like Ian Chappell, he's moulded Western Province into a side from virtually nothing. That intense belief in himself rubs off on the players, they believe in Barlow, and as a result of the way he builds each of his players up, they soon come to believe in themselves. He'll do anything for his side. If someone has the audacity to criticise any member of his side, he'll argue the toss for hours. So Western Province is a bubbly side, and that can't be bad.

If South Africa picked a Test side now, I have no doubts that Barlow would be captain. That would be great for the game. Like Richards, Pollock, and Procter, Barlow's Test career has been shamefully cut short. Hopefully he'll achieve one of his greatest ambitions and lead South Africa out into a Test

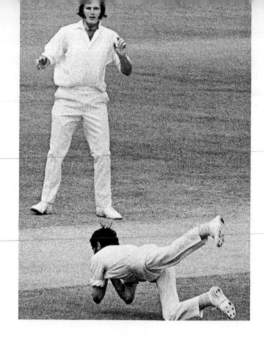

Bevan Congdon *has done a fantastic job for New Zealand*

An unusual combination. *Rarely does an all-out aggressive speedster double up as a great batsman, except Procter*

match wearing the famous Springbok cap. That was something Basil d'Oliveira could never have done, though he did so with honour for England.

Born in Cape Town, Basil's a cape coloured and his is probably the all-time great Cinderella story of international cricket. It's a long way from the back streets of Cape Town to Buckingham Palace. If ever a class cricketer was brought up with the odds stacked against him, then Basil d'Oliveira was the one. His bestselling autobiography, *The d'Oliveira Story*, was bought by huge numbers of non-cricket lovers, as well as many who know the game well. For it wasn't just written by a wellknown cricketer, it told a fairy story of his climb out of the wilderness and little hope, right to the top of the international cricket tree. That's a huge haul.

D'Oliveira's success was summed up in that book which was read by the old ladies in the same way they might read a sentimental novel. There was nothing controversial in it, only straightforward facts of the hard road he'd travelled, the pitfalls, the joys. Above all, Basil has maintained dignity, even though he has far more axes to grind than someone like anti-apartheid activist Peter Hain. Now his career is finished, d'Oliveira can stand up and be counted. A credit to South Africa, in every way he's been a true sportsman who has always had nothing but praise for his birthplace, never militant in his thinking. I cannot give him recognition in this book for the man he is off the field, even though he's worth so much on his own. But as a jack-of-all trades, d'Oliveira was a true crisis man for England, in every department.

The cynics over the years have said, 'How

Doug Walters. *An idol in Sydney and a great player on his day anywhere in the world*

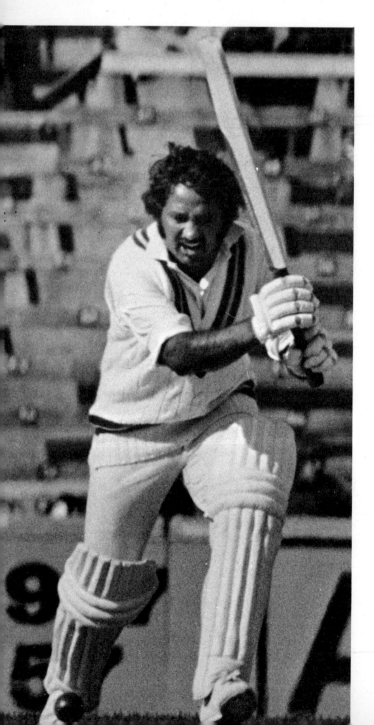

Mushtaq Mohammad, *the full range of shots*

can a man with his poor background, ever make it at a packed Lord's in a crisis against the arch-enemy, Australia?' Made it he did and more. For Basil had trodden the hard road and the memory was deeply embedded. Having made it as a Test cricketer, and as his bread and butter, there was absolutely no way that he was going to fail for that could have meant a return to the past.

Even though he made a late start in life as an international cricketer, he made the grade as a batsman with patience, a tremendous medium-pacer, and a very useful fieldsman. He wasn't as athletic as Sobers, Lloyd, Bland or Sheahan in their heyday, but even now d'Oliveira has a magnificent arm from the boundary, flat and hard, straight over the top of the bails.

He has proved to be a tremendously strong man. When he hits the ball it stays hit. In fact he is one of the hardest hitters of the ball I've ever seen. Dolly and I share the same view on how to treat a crisis. Both of us take the attitude that attack is the best means of defence, and we'd far rather smash the ball than shut up shop and potter around hoping for a miracle.

There's nothing rash in such an attitude, it's more like taking the initiative away from the bowler, and letting him worry about the consequences. Former England captain Ray Illingworth never handed out praise at random, yet he states that d'Oliveira with bat and ball was one of the major reasons why he was a successful Test captain.

Many a time Illingworth would call on d'Oliveira in a tight situation that required tight bowling and not only would he fill that bill, but take wickets as well. His very

Greg Chappell, *he doesn't bowl enough*

deceptive action and easy approach foiled many a class batsman, and because of his strength his faster ball was mighty quick, with no apparent change in delivery. In some ways he's a bit like Jeff Thomson, purely in principle and not in pace.

I will always remember dropping a slips catch off Basil at Manchester against Australia, because I badly misread his quicker ball. There was no way I could have caught it. D'Oliveira's quicker ball was the danger one, it seemed to come out of nowhere. In that instance I was perhaps five yards too close, and it hit me before I saw it.

Basil d'Oliveira's a quiet, efficient guy who just got on with the job. Only after the day's play he would open up, and he had a great sense of humour. Early in my Test career I was chosen to play against the Rest of the World at Headingley, with Basil. To me that was a great honour. Here were two South African-born all-rounders playing for England, one white and one coloured, something we both wished would happen in South Africa. Basil still coaches coloureds there at every chance.

We were both sitting together getting changed on the first day when Geoff Boycott came into the room while we were nattering to one another in Afrikaans. That in itself was quite funny, for nobody had any idea of what we were talking about. Geoff made a funny comment, although to some it might not seem so. But it was funny, because Geoff has spent many an English winter's coaching, like Basil, in South Africa. Said 'Fiery', 'I hate to think what Vorster would say if he knew I was playing in the same side as you two'. Some of the side gave an embarrassed giggle, others thought—as Basil and I did—that it was just a plain joke.

Basically, I was a little bit shy in those days, to me it was still a big, new world. 'Fiery' went straight through the room into the toilet after finishing his remark and one or two of the lads said not to let him get away with that, but pull his leg and get stuck into him right away. They geed me up to follow Geoff into the toilet for a word or two. Jokingly, but in a serious manner I told him, 'It was very, very embarrassing to be in the side with a coloured when I'm white, and I'm finding it difficult enough without such comments from you'. Naturally, Geoff swallowed it hook, line and sinker. Everyone in the team remained silent, tongue in cheek, when I returned. Basil then went up to Geoff and said, 'Give the young bloke a go, he's just arrived in the side and it's a very difficult situation for him to be in'. A few of the others lent their voices to the act, and everyone other than 'Fiery' was laughing up their sleeve.

Geoff didn't say another word that day, and the next morning he arrived very early at the ground and waited for me. He led me into the physio room and said, 'Look Greigy, I want to apologise profusely for causing you any embarrassment. I've been to South Africa many times, and I know what you mean. I'm really sorry. Don't for God's sake think I was being hurtful, I just thought it was a joke'.

I managed for about two minutes to say something about not thinking he was as thoughtless as that, but I couldn't contain myself, and burst out laughing. Naturally 'Fiery' knew right there and then that he'd been taken for a ride, but it was a great start for me with Geoff. From that point on we never stopped taking the mickey out of one another. That was healthy, and proved to be

87

Basil d'Oliveira, *the all-time Cinderella story of international cricket*

Basil, *a tremendous medium pacer*

beneficial much later on when we did come to grips. We were on common ground, and respected each other for it.

My last great all-rounder is Illingworth, and he goes one step further than the rest, in quantity. For he's the best captain I've ever played under and, like d'Oliveira, a reliable crisis man.

Illingworth's the complete cricketer. As a bowler, his off-spinners were tight and tidy, yet he could attack if necessary. His bowling was in keeping with his tactical thinking as a captain, without doubt the best tactician I've seen.

In a Sydney Test most of the side thought John Snow and Peter Lever were going to win it for England late in the game, but Illingworth shared the ball with Underwood, and England won handsomely to regain the Ashes. As a batsman, Illingworth scored many runs batting at six or seven, and in my time was one of the few batsmen who could successfully hook.

As a fieldsman Illingworth could cover any position. I came in on the tail-end of his career, when he wasn't quite as agile as before. Nevertheless, anywhere from first slip to around the corner Illingworth was class, especially in the bat-pad position, surely one of the toughest to shine in. He could slot into any spot and do it well. His record as an all-rounder is in the top five of all time in England, so it speaks for itself.

So to do the job he did as a player, and head my list as a captain as well, ensures Illingworth's place among my top five jacks-of-all-trades. I've learned so much from him. He's only too willing to talk about why he did such and such, backing up his judgement with examples and reasons. He is that sort of

I'm fortunate. If the wicket isn't seaming, I can turn to off spinners to stay involved

captain, a very logical man who based his decisions on fact, never fiction. He was never a Sobers, but in every department of the game he was indeed the complete cricketer.

That brings me to those all-rounders who haven't made the top five, but who for one reason or another certainly rate honourable mention. The closest to the top is Greg Chappell, Australia's new Test captain. Had Chappell bowled more I have no doubt he would have rated far higher. In England, we have a healthy regard for his bowling. Happily for us he didn't bowl too often.

There's no doubting his ability, but maybe he doesn't like bowling too much in case it affects his magnificent batting. But Chappell can bowl anything to suit the conditions. I'd sooner face Doug Walters than Chappell, even though Walters has proved very successful.

Chappell can go right through the card— little in and outswingers, he also slips in a leg cutter and a slower ball, and I've seen him bowl spells of fastish off-breaks, wrapping his fingers around the ball on a slow English turner.

His record as a batsman needs no introduction, he is a superb player, while his fielding can be just out of this world in any position. Proof enough is his world record. Seven catches in the second Test at Perth against us in 1974 taken all around the field. Now he has the job of captaining Australia, it will be interesting to see how he treats himself as a bowler.

Australia's Gary Gilmour would romp into the top category if he ever puts his mind to it. Here's a youngster with immense ability who all too often goes to sleep on it. Admittedly he's relatively inexperienced, but to me that's

no excuse for an all-out effort at every opportunity.

Gilmour has the lot. He was unplayable in two games at Headingley—the Prudential World Cup semi-final against us when he ripped right through to capture 6–14 off his maximum twelve overs, and again the third Test where he backed up with 6–85 off 31.2 overs of sustained swing bowling. Yet in between there have been far too many times when he's not let himself go.

He's one of only three left-arm medium-pacers that I've seen who can move the ball either way in the air. This ability is a rarity. The others are Sobers and West Indian team-mate Bernard Julien.

Gilmour's batting can be electric. He is certainly a powerhouse as one of the hardest hitters in the game, but he doesn't get enough runs. As with his bowling, Gilmour doesn't put it all together often enough in keeping with his ability. As a fieldsman he's brilliant and possesses a tracer-bullet arm from the deepest outfield.

To me it's all a matter of application. At the moment Gary Gilmour hasn't applied himself regularly enough. When he does he'll be at the top of the current crop of international all-rounders. Gilmour has so much to offer the game, but it must be fully utilised.

Julien is so much like Gilmour, but because he's had more experience, his performances are a little more consistent. Besides his ability to move the ball either way, he has a slower ball, a really good bouncer, and if he ever gets stuck right into the game he'll also reach the top. His batting and fielding follow the Gilmour pattern.

One innings of Julien's I'll never forget was at Lord's. It was a blazing century, one of

Intikhab Alam, *a great leg spinner, and a batsman who can turn a game in a matter of overs*

those knocks where chaps who play the way Julien—a right-hander—and Gilmour—a left-hander—do, go out and give the ball one hell of a smack. Julien did not put a foot wrong that day in one of the best innings I've ever seen, playing almost every shot. The two of them have another thing in common, they premeditate their shots and obviously that gets them into strife.

Even though he's not fast, Julien quite often gets the new ball for the West Indies ahead of faster men like Keith Boyce and Vanburn Holder, because of his ability to swing it so much. As a fieldsman, Julien is like so many West Indians, although I wouldn't rate him as anything out of the box.

Team-mate Boyce deserves to be rated. He's an aggressive cricketer with bat and ball, and has one of the strongest arms in the game. He's more a bowler-all-rounder, than a batsman-all-rounder. He screams into the wicket and the many pictures of Boyce just after delivering the ball aptly prove the point. You would think he'd have to fall over, so angled to the ground is his body at that stage.

Boyce loves bowling bouncers, and he bowls them well. He has a good outswinger, but it's his aggression and strength that pull him through. As a batsman he finds himself in the lower order because of the make-up of the West Indian Test line-up, but he smashes the living daylights out of the ball. Limited-over cricket is tailormade for him, he's a good all-rounder.

I bracket Pakistanis Intikhab Alam and Mushtaq Mohammad together. Inti is a leg-break bowler cum-batsman, Mushtaq the opposite. I have already rated Inti as a leg spinner, the best in the world in my time.

A slap-happy batsman, Inti can turn a game in a matter of overs. Mushtaq, the youngest Test cricketer in history, has played many great innings for his country and for County Northamptonshire. He has a full range of shots, and a determination that seems to be part and parcel of the incredible Mohammad family which has provided five first-class cricketers. Older brother Hanif still holds the world individual batting record of 499, so records run in the family. Neither Inti nor Mushtaq are great fieldsmen, but they are more than adequate.

Asif Iqbal, another Pakistani, is a brilliant fieldsman, fast with a good arm. That's the strongest part of his game, but he's been very successful with Pakistan and Kent with bat and ball. As a batsman, the slightly-built Asif hits the ball hard, and is always a big danger.

Doug Walters is like Iqbal in many ways, bowls much the same, and can field in any position. He has been a much maligned cricketer over the years, but he's served Australia well.

There have been any number of times when scribes and spectators alike have called for Walter's dismissal from the Test side, although you wouldn't hear that in Sydney, where he is worshipped. Early in his career he looked like a world-beater. After two successive centuries in his first two Tests, he became the first batsman to score a double and a single century in the one Test. The first record was against England, the second against the West Indies, and he's topped them off with four different centuries in a session so far in his career. In the meantime he's averaged nearly 50, but I've often wondered whether or not he's really applied himself.

Bernard Julien *has all the makings of a great all-rounder, but needs more application*

Walters has to rely on a great eye to fire, technically he has many flaws. On good wickets he can get away with a looser game. That's why he hasn't really played so well in England, where the ball does more off the wicket—the flaws have been found more easily and he couldn't adjust. He's a renowned partnership breaker with his medium-pacers, doing just a little here and there, strangling out good batsmen often, and he's in the top bracket as far as fielding is concerned, anywhere from slips to the outfield. His arm is safe and sure, even though it's not over-strong. There's no doubting Doug Walters is an Australian asset.

New Zealand's Bevan Congdon is in the same class. I have already recognised him as a world-class workhorse, but that takes second place to his batting and captaincy. As a batsman Congdon showed the way in many series, and in a side that wasn't strong. He led from the front, and his two 170s against us in 1973 were solid knocks of immense worth.

Congdon, like most New Zealanders, suffered from inconsistent international competition. Nevertheless, he made his own way through sheer determination and for that he's got to be admired. Maybe his captaincy bordered on the negative, but he could hardly be on the all-out attack with such a fragile side.

As a fieldsman Congdon was safe, not spectacular, and in fact that sums up Bevan Congdon pretty well—safe. He's done a great job for New Zealand.

India hasn't been blessed with too many all-rounders, but in Eknath Solkar they've found one who's done the trick often. Solkar's not a great player by any means, although he's the greatest bat-pad fieldsman I've ever seen. In that department alone there's none better, but as a batsman and a bowler he's had his moments when India were in strife.

Solkar has done as much for India as anyone. He had a golden run against the West Indies and England when India were right on top. He can bowl left-arm seamers or orthodox spinners, feature in the middle batting order and has the best temperament in the side. I've seen India in situations they would never have recovered from without Solkar.

In England there are two I rate—the newcomer Bob Woolmer and the more experienced Chris Old.

I think Woolmer will make the grade more as a batsman. He's already made a big hundred against Australia in the last Test at The Oval, and that takes some doing. He bowls tidy medium-pacers and can field anywhere. But he has time on his side, and I'm looking for big things from him in the future. Old's made his name as one of England's top seamers and there have been times when he's bowled very fast. He can field anywhere and has a good arm, but his batting has been a disappointment.

Old has scored a first-class century, but he should be averaging between 30 and 40 each season. The ability is there, that's for certain, all it needs is more application.

So I've covered the best in the jacks-of-all-trades department. They play a major role in any team effort, providing the vital extra depth that lifts an ordinary side into a good one.

8

The Men in Gloves
The Wicket-Keepers

I left wicket-keepers out of the chapter on the all-rounders, even though every one of the current Test Keepers bats as well.

I have often been asked who is the best keeper in the world, Knott or Marsh? I'll probably be accused of being biased, but my vote would have to go to Knott. Maybe because I've seen Knott so much more—over forty Test matches and countless County and limited-over games—I'm in a better position to judge him.

So Alan Knott takes top billing, but right here and now I can only sing the highest praise of Rod Marsh. When he first came onto the scene, replacing Brian Taber in the 1970–71 series against England in Australia, Marsh quickly picked up the tab of 'Iron Gloves'.

Marsh punched the ball all round the place, and seemed hopelessly out of condition with a very bulky physique. Admittedly he had some difficult bowling to keep to, but nevertheless he was never ever in the race when it came to any comparison with Knott or any other of the top keepers of the day. But how he's worked at his game. It's absolutely incredible how much he's improved on those early days to become one of the great keepers, there is now no doubt of that. So the frontrunner is Knott. I've never, ever seen him bad, right from the word go. Sure he's made a few mistakes here and there, but over so many Test matches it's hardly been noticed.

Knott is only proud of feats. If a day goes by without him being noticed, something is wrong, and yet he is so modest, one of the greatest guys I have had the pleasure to play

with. He's a perfectionist, a fitness fanatic, a great keeper. But Knotty thrives on being criticised. That may sound rather strange, but to Knott that makes the difference between knowing and not knowing where he is going wrong, and gives him ideas on what to work on, because he never stops working at his game. Second-best doesn't rate with Knott, he's got to be at the top of the tree.

No doubt that's one of the major reasons why he's been so good for so long. We are good for each other. I know very little about keeping, Knott knows a lot about bowling, after all he's kept to so many great bowlers. Therefore I treat what he says with respect and he respects what I say about his keeping. While we are in the slips together there's a banter between us that keeps both of us on our toes.

Cricket's a funny game, depending on the make-up of those concerned. There are quite a few players who can't take criticism, whether it's really meant, or just a rib here and there. Knotty and I are motivated from the word go, but a choice word here and there from one to another brings out the best in each of us. If, at the end of the day there have been two byes, Knott will look back and say to himself, 'Why?' and he'll work it out.

Knott's concentration is also unbelievable. He gets down, at the very latest, as the bowler starts his run and from that moment on he's the epitome of intense concentration. He greatly values his standing among the world's keepers, and jealously guards his reputation. There's no way Knott would pick up the MCC coaching manual. What applies as a general rule doesn't necessarily apply to Alan Knott. Knott does his job his way, the same applies to

The top two keepers: *Alan Knott, the batsman, watched by Rod Marsh*

Marsh the batsman *watched by Alan Knott*

Typical Knott. *Having dived full length, Knott comes up with another outstanding catch*

Next page

Mobility Marsh. *Dubbed the "catch of the year", Marsh catches Clive Lloyd at Perth in a World XI game, 1971*

A diving save. *Rod Marsh dives down the leg side to save off Dennis Lillee's bowling against Pakistan at Sydney, 1973*

his batting, and many a time he's saved England from disaster.

Here's a man who defies the coaching manual with the bat as well. His square-on stance is completely unorthodox, but very effective. That's been very handy for Knott. Being a crisis man has insured his place in England's Test side, despite Derbyshire's Bob Taylor constantly pressing him as a keeper.

Knott is always keen to learn. I remember him asking me about my lifting cuts over the slips at Brisbane on the way to my first century against Australia last tour. So it came as no surprise when Knotty did the same thing at Adelaide in the fifth Test to notch his first ton against Australia—an unbeaten one at that as wickets fell all around him. This was a replica of my innings. He raced through the eighties and nineties and on to the hundred off Dennis Lillee, doing the same thing as I had done in Brisbane. When he came off the field he sat down in the corner, caught my eye, and gave me a big wink as if to say what a good idea.

So there's no doubt Knott's a thinker, so too was Colin Cowdrey. At Perth, Kipper had been hit all over the place and was struggling in his first game for months, having been called into the side after the tour started, when we were plagued by so many injuries. This had gone on for two hours for Cowdrey. I came in to be greeted by a bouncer which I flashed at and hit over slips' head, the next one I middled over gully for four with no third man and Cowdrey came down the wicket and said, 'Interesting, interesting'. There's no way Kipper would have followed suit, it wasn't in his make up to drastically change his batting technique that was so close

to the manual. Not so Knott. If he could see someway, however unorthodox, that he could score more runs or take more catches, then he would try it, and try it in the middle where it really counts.

As a fellow all-round, Alan Knott could be one of my frontrunners, both as a keeper-batsman and as a bloke. But despite all Knott's good points, he has a permanent problem. He is so meticulous when it comes to health, even down to cleaning his teeth umpteen times a day, and packing his kit bag presents any amount of problems. Never can it be closed first time, it requires a superhuman effort to latch it shut. Even then, bits and pieces of clothing hang out of it. It is chock full of gear, bats, pads, gloves, whatever. The main reason again is his ultra-cleanliness.

Every time he comes off the field Knotty changes his clothes. You can imagine how many sets of creams that involves, and little wonder why his bag is damned hard to close. Without his wife he's utterly hopeless. He can't sew on a button, and that's why you so often see him looking scruffy on the field. He'll happily safety-pin or sticking-plaster his shirt or pants together and there's always a multitude of dry cleaning tags spread around his motel room. As for his keeping gloves, they are treated like Royalty. He always has a favourite pair which he treasures, and always has a reserve pair that get a terrible hiding every night with a bat handle, just in case the main pair splits. He's continuously working on the other pair to break them in so that they are as close to the main pair as possible.

The health kick goes further than teeth. Knotty won't eat potatoes with steak and in Australia especially that's hard not to do. He

reckons that those foods don't combine well unless they're eaten separately and therefore aren't in his best interests. To go even further, sweets aren't eaten until at least half an hour after his main course, that must be digested first. In India Knott comes unstuck. You'll see him drinking a bottle of soft drink, and hating every minute of it because he can't drink the water.

Wherever possible Knotty is given his own room on tour. He's up at the crack of dawn exercising, just as he does on the field, every ball. Alan Knott's best summed up by saying he does everything properly, right down to the last full stop. That would drive a lot of people mad, but you completely accept it in the little keeper, he's just that sort of bloke. And, to prove the point, I've never been to an England selection meeting as captain without first phoning up Alan Knott. To me he's all that's good in the game, as a competitor, as a player and as a thinker. I value his opinions, and that's why I wanted him as my vice-captain. And he would not let me down in a million years.

That brings me to Marsh, who really is on a par with my number one. But you can only have one top keeper, though Rodney Marsh has my highest commendation for shedding four stone in weight and working on his forte to such an extent as to lift himself from the bottom rung of international keepers to the pinnacle.

I've already talked about Gilmour and Julien, two highly talented players who haven't got around to mastering untold natural ability. Marsh hasn't anywhere near the same natural ability as those two, but has he ever worked on what he's got! From a punching keeper and slap-happy batsman, Marsh has raced into the record books with many superb displays in both departments. What's more, he's also a good thinker. When Ian Chappell retired as Australia's Test captain I asked him (Ian Chappell), who he thought would take over. He replied that there were three possibilities. That surprised me. I had pencilled in Greg Chappell and Ian Redpath, both agreed to by Chappell, who also added Rod Marsh.

Surprise is an understatement. Here was a man who had so changed his game that he could bat aggressively or play the dour role if it was required. That was a far cry from the Rod Marsh of early days and his keeping also went ahead in leaps and bounds.

His batting has been invaluable to Australia. First up, if he got to 40 or 50 you knew, really knew, that that was the limit and he'd very soon give his innings away. Nowadays, if Marsh gets to 50, you've really got to worry how to stop him getting to 100, or even further. That's tremendous credit to Marsh. Knott was always good from the beginning, he never had to go on the big improvement campaign to succeed as a keeper, only to achieve some tidying up as a batsman. Marsh had to work on both, and he's done it magnificently well. What more can you say about Marsh than that?

I have no doubts that Marsh's fierce competitive nature has been instilled by Ian Chappell over the years. Marsh has many a word to say on the field, but off it he's a different bloke. I've been to two Aussie Test players' homes, Marsh's and Ross Edwards'. At home Marsh is quiet and a pleasure to talk to about the game. He's vastly different on the

Farokh Engineer *in position should I miss a square cut at Lord's in 1974*

Next page

Majid Khan. *The Pakistani just misses David Lloyd on his way to 98 at Lord's in 1974*

field, but that's nothing against him. To the contrary, it's to be commended in many ways.

Yet there have been times when Marsh has been a very short-tempered player—like a lot of Australians, his rage shows through. At Edgbaston he broke the glass dressing-room door in anger, but you can bet that five minutes later he was back to his easy-going self, whereas someone like Geoff Boycott would wander around the room for hours with his pads on after suffering the same sort of fate. This has all become part and parcel of Test cricket, followed ball by ball by at least four television cameras. They don't miss much—the hinges on the Headingley dressing room door will be a topic of conversation long after Ian Chappell had vented his feelings after being given out in that third Test against England in 1975.

While I'm on the subject, I think it's time more players gave some thought to their public attitude. I hasten to add that ninety nine times out of a hundred Ian Chappell would be given out and just go. He accepts umpires' decisions. The Leeds episode was a one out, but it made an impact and a half. I've been guilty of a couple myself, but I believed that I had to stop for the sake of the game and the thousands of youngsters who watch, and then take off any antics they see on their own field.

Had Rod Marsh taken over the captaincy he'd probably have got to the situation where he would, like me, look back and say, 'Why the hell did I do that?'

So from a quiet keeper and an explosive one, back to the quietest of the lot, Pakistan's Wasim Bari. Knott rates Wasim and Marsh together, and I'd almost go along with that.

There are no over-actions with Wasim, neither the constant Knott-type calisthenics nor the ultra-aggressive Marsh. Wasim just goes about his job with the barest minimum of fuss.

Wasim and Bob Taylor could be bracketed together in this regard. It's very hard to go into any depth about either of them, except to say both are fine keepers and Wasim the far better batsman. Admittedly, Taylor hasn't been fully tested in the Test match arena, he's the constant touring bridesmaid to Knott. But a better team man you could not find. He'll work like a slave at the nets, be out early to help Knott warm up, and generally be a Man Friday to everyone in the side. He just can't do enough for his team-mates. He's invaluable on tour, despite being always in the background. Many have rated Taylor a better keeper than Knott, but a far inferior batsman. That's a major reason why Knotty has ruled the roost, apart from one Test against New Zealand that was given to Taylor for his countless services rendered. Knott was asked to stand down, but on reflection now I think he's sorry he did it, thus breaking a massive run of successive Tests. I couldn't possibly be in the background like Taylor for that long without giving it away. That's one of the reasons why I have such admiration for him. It was only justice to see him appointed captain of Derbyshire last season.

Wasim would fit into any side with no problems. He takes all bowlers with ease, and his swift movements behind the stumps are barely noticed, so unobtrusively does he do his job. But cometh the edge, and you can count your lucky stars if Wasim grasses it, he's so safe and has lightning-fast reflexes.

In support: *the Chappell brothers set off to back up Ian Redpath at Brisbane in 1975. There was no need, for Redpath took the catch to dismiss Inshan Ali off the bowling of Jeff Thomson*

Below

Sarfraz Nawaz. *Watched by Aftab Gul and batsman Glenn Turner, Sarfraz puts everything into this Prudential World Cup clash*

The pain of it all. *Ken Wadsworth collects one midstream on his way to a century for South Island against the West Indies in 1969. The phlegmatic slip is Rohan Kanhai*

Next comes India's Farokh Engineer, the conductor of the glovemen. At home Farokh gees up the crowd to his side's own benefit, often claiming a wicket through a thoroughly good Oscar-winning performance. Picture him as chief conductor to 70,000 at Calcutta or 75,000 at Bombay, purely by raising his arms up high, as if in appeal. He only appeals when he thinks it may be out, but when he raises his arms, up goes the entire crowd—imagine the din.

He doesn't half create pressure in India for England, not half. Every time you play and miss and the whole crowd goes 'Ooo. .aah', it does give you many a heart stop, believe me.

Farokh doesn't rate as highly as the other three, yet while he's an orthodox keeper, he's an unorthodox batsman, and highly effective. He has opened the batting for India and the World XI in Tests and batted down the order, both with a lot of success. He generally throws caution to the wind, relying on a good eye and a smattering of good fortune. But fortune favours the brave, and Engineer's been brave most of the time. He loves to drive, cut and hook, rarely getting into position, but more often than not middling the ball. He'll drag even a half volley outside off stump through the on side, then laugh. He can't cover drive at all. Farokh has been well and truly tested at international level. He kept to the best pacemen in the first World XI series in England and in Tests has to contend with the champion Indian spinners on raging turners, so he's a very fine cricketer.

In his off-field moments, Farokh sells blankets—a hard sell at that. We always have a laugh about it when he brings up the subject in India, as he always will. It's so damned hot

there that you need a blanket like a hole in the head. But that doesn't deter Farokh and it's typical, too, of the way he plays his cricket, he never gives in.

Deryck Murray has had a great influence on West Indian cricket, and it's fitting that he's now vice-captain to the effervescent Clive Lloyd. Murray is a tidy keeper, and a very useful batsman. He doesn't rate with either Knott or Marsh, but rarely does he do anything wrong, and he's as quiet as a mouse on the field. But he's highly efficient, and a great team man. As a batsman he can be a huge nuisance. Pakistan found that out in the Prudential World Cup series game when Murray assisted Vanburn Holder and Andy Roberts to add 101 runs for the loss of only Holder to beat Pakistan by one wicket. Murray finished with 61 not out, and it reminded me of a magnificent century he scored in the initial World XI series in England, opening the batting.

Like Engineer, Murray is a very versatile batsman, yet he plays more as a bonus for his partner than anything else. Man can he hit! Yet he does it relatively safely, lofting the ball only into wide open spaces. Nothing affects him. I recall the game against Trinidad in 1974 where Deryck was captain. I bowled him a ball that literally shot along the deck as he played back. His foot would have been only six inches from the middle stump and an appeal was a mere formality and it was first ball as well.

Having appealed, I just wandered down the wicket before coming to a grinding halt as I realised there wasn't too much activity from the umpire. Deryck looked at me rather sheepishly, and his goatee beard was twitch-

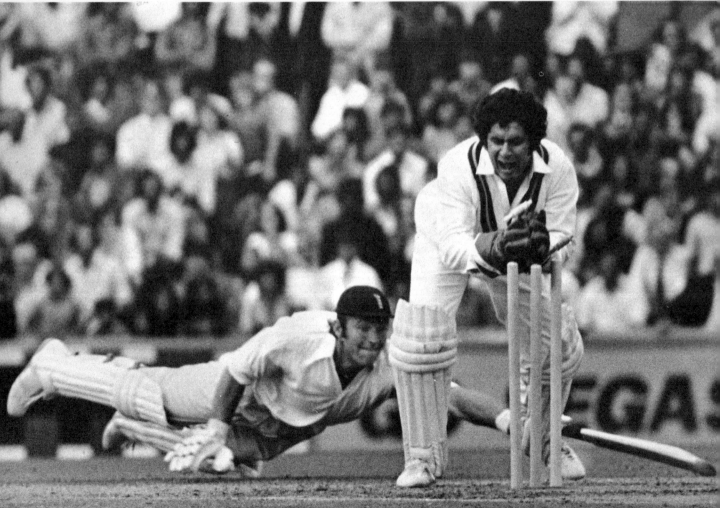

Jubilation. *Burgess dismissed Trent Bridge, 1973. Ray Illingworth, Keith Fletcher, Alan Knott and I appeal*

Wasim Bari: *the return was just a fraction late to run out a desperate Dennis Amiss. This photograph was one of a series that won Ken Kelly the 1974 British Sports Photographer of the Year award*

Keeper takes keeper. *Deryck Murray holds aloft the chance given by Alan Knott off Keith Boyce at Lord's, 1973*

ing with embarrassment. But it sure didn't worry him for too long as he smashed his way to over 150! Murray has been a tough competitor for Warwickshire in County cricket—and will no doubt serve the Windies well for a long time.

I have tremendous admiration for Ken Wadsworth, last, but by no means least, of the current crop of international keepers. Many a time the hard-hitting Wadsworth has saved New Zealand. Most of those innings came at a time when New Zealand was in dire straits, so he's proved to be a crisis man. But in many ways he's like Gilmour and Julien—stacks of ability not fully utilised. True, he's played many fine innings for his country, and under intense pressure, but I've always had the feeling that he's a better player than it shows on paper. Perhaps he would be more successful in a better side. Admittedly it's a lot more difficult to fire regularly in a side that tends to crumble too often, but all the ingredients are there for Wadsworth to make the grade as a Test batsman alone if he only constantly applied himself.

As a keeper I couldn't class him with the others, but he's generally safe, and has snapped up some great catches. But the same applies to his keeping as with the bat. He's the tallest of the Test keepers, and therefore takes more out of himself through a day in the field.

He takes the ball smoothly, yet when his concentration starts to fade, he tends to go to pieces and that's where he gets into trouble. More's the pity, for he hasn't done himself justice. Any keeper who just pads the ball away when he's tired instead of stooping to catch it has a way to go before he makes the top grade.

Although he hasn't yet made Test status, I must mention Australia's second-string keeper to England, Richie Robinson. Like Taylor, Robinson was only too happy to help his team mates. He roomed with Jeff Thomson, and offered his services without being asked to help Thomson in any way. Robinson would pack Thomson's bag, see that everything was shipshape, be one of the first to nets and the last to leave So keen is Robinson that he has stated he would work hard on his batting and try to make the Test side as a batsman. That's true dedication and the way Robinson attacks the game, it's not beyond the realms of possibility.

So there are the world's keepers and they all have something in common, they are all-rounders. Not one of the current Test keepers hasn't made his mark as a batsman as well, so it appears that this has now become a prerequisite.

That can't be bad, for as I've said before the perfect team would be five of the best batsmen and five of the best bowlers in the world and a keeper who can bat. This is the era of keeper-batsmen, and I hope it never changes, for it's good for the game.

9

The Men in Charge

The Great Captains

Good Test captains are hard to come by, great ones are rare. So it's strange that in my era there are two who have attained the top bracket and been consistently classed as great. They are Ray Illingworth of England and Australia's Ian Chappell.

I've said before the Illingworth is tops. In some ways that may sound hard on Chappell, who has led Australia so well for a record-breaking thirty Tests, one ahead of Bobby Simpson and two better than Richie Benaud. But Illy had everything. Of course, it's a lot easier to judge a man's ability in any area when you've played so much under him—and against him. I've seen Illingworth in good times and bad, and never has he given any impression other than that of being totally in command.

Great captains read a game in advance, even make something happen that will be to their benefit, and are all-round psychologists. Illingworth was England's Test captain when I arrived on the scene and the factor that stood out in my mind was that he was so technically sound. As an all-rounder himself, Illingworth knew all the pros and cons of batsmen, bowlers and fieldsmen. More than most he could appreciate what made them tick. That insight meant a lot to Illingworth. It allowed him to shift from one line of thinking to another without changing gear himself.

Deep down, his tough Yorkshire background held him in good stead as well. Up there they were so used to winning that Illingworth worked overtime to ensure the same applied to any side he captained from that point on. It didn't matter whether it was England or later Leicestershire, whom he recently led to their first County champion-ship in history, the principle was the same. At all times you had the impression Illingworth had a thoroughly professional outlook and always had something up his sleeve. Therefore he was always so much in command. He didn't shout, nor was he quiet. Verbally, he was middle-of-the-road, but every word he said meant something and he expected, without qualification, his word would be carried out.

Illingworth has had some tough areas to get through, not the easiest of which was the 1970–71 tour to Australia, when it has been said the English camp was split in two. Yet on the field Illy handled them all and kept them all together to such an extent that England won back the Ashes against all odds. That was a brilliant exhibition of captaincy.

Right from the outset of that tour Illingworth was under a cloud, he was on a hiding to nothing unless he won. The appointment of David Clark as manager was in anticipation of Cowdrey being made captain. Whether that was right or not was immaterial in the net result, for Illingworth saw to it that all, and I mean all, his players were motivated.

That's why the side was so successful. At one stage Snow was in his best 'hard to handle' mood, something I understand but cope with at Sussex, but it wasn't in the best interests of the side in Australia. And even though Snowie was the spearhead of the attack, Illingworth told him what was expected of him, showed him his return flight to England ticket, and advised him to go away for a couple of hours and think about it. This happened before the first Test, and the records show that Snowie accepted the ultimatum and virtually won the series on his

The symbol of success: my top captain does it again. Ray Illingworth holds aloft the coveted Benson and Hedges Cup after Leicester had beaten Middlesex at Lord's in 1975

own with some devastating bowling. Because Snow, d'Oliveira and Boycott all so respected Illingworth, even though there were times when they possibly thought he was being a bit tough, so much was to be gained by not bucking the system.

In my own case, I played for England against the Rest of the World in 1970, was dropped because I wasn't what Illingworth wanted at that stage, then was recalled. Yet I missed the 1970–71 tour to Australia, and after making my mark in the World XI tour there the following year I was back in the England side, again under Illingworth.

Once I'd made the grade, Illy would never let me down as long as I gave him a hundred per cent. I knew it, and that meant a lot to me as my confidence grew with every Test. Despite the setbacks and bitter disappointments we all go through at Test level, Illingworth at all times was my man at the helm, and whatever he wanted was all right by me because I believed in him. That's how much I respected him, and that feeling will never change.

Illingworth had everything under control, and I don't know one player who doesn't respect him as a captain. He was obviously a player's captain. He would do anything to back them up, even in little things like meal allowances. The very first evening meal I had with the Test side, Illy had a normal three-course evening meal and a glass of beer. Adding up the bill, it came to more than our allowance.

He walked straight over to the manager, laid the bill out on the table, and quietly pointed out that the allowance did not cover a normal meal and should therefore be increased for every player. This was done and appreciated by those of us who had just come into his side, because never in a million years would any of us have dared to suggest it at that stage in our careers.

Illy not only justified his own selection as a player by continually taking wickets, scoring runs and snapping up catches—above all that he kept a side motivated and in search of victory, clash of personalities or not. As a player under his captaincy all you had to do was your own job, he had the rest covered. He spelt it all out clearly, and away you'd go.

The closest to Illingworth was Ian Chappell, a great fighter and a great moulder of men. He started with an ordinary side, smartly whipping them into a hard to beat unit.

There's a lot in common between Illingworth and Chappell. Both were nonconformists to a degree and therefore in a way were looked upon as anti-administration. There was only one basic difference between them in this area. Illy was sacked as Test captain, Chappell got out before the axe fell.

The Chappell saga will live forever nevertheless, be it good or bad. I have nothing but the highest admiration for the man and have thoroughly enjoyed my few tussles with him. He has tried absolutely everything to put me off my game, to rattle me, and I've done the same thing. It never ends. I played a couple of charity games at Sydney's Drummoyne Oval early this season and it was still on.

Chappell has one habit of raising his arms, bat and all, mimicking me after I reckon I've bowled him a jaffa. He did it again at Drummoyne and first ball at that. Having made his point he killed himself laughing,

Ian Chappell, a great leader from the front, on his way to 192 in his last Test as Australian captain, The Oval, 1975

The end of an era. *Chappell departs after his 192, an innings so typically dedicated to his team effort*

To get his wicket always gives me immense satisfaction. But it has never given me greater pleasure than in the final Test of our 1974 to 1975 tour to Australia at Melbourne. In that game I dismissed him in both innings, caught down the leg side on each occasion. Both times, Ian gave the impression that he did not think he was out, but I was convinced that he had got a touch and delighted to claim a double success over a man I considered a great player and a tremendous rival. Perhaps our clashes on the pitch have sometimes become heated, but I honestly believe that is out of respect for each other. On this occasion there was no armwaving from me because our manager, Alec Bedser, had warned me that my habit of pointing to the pavilion was out of order. I got all the satisfaction I needed just watching Ian disappearing into the pavilion for the second time.

But what I like about Chappell is that no matter what happens on the field it's all over and done with after the day's play. I don't begrudge anyone who plays it really hard in the centre. What I can't stand are players who carry their anger into the night, maybe right through a five-day Test. To me the day's play is done, and it's time for a beer and a chat about what's happened or whatever. That's one of the best times of the day.

I've yet to hear one Australian player shower anything but praise on Ian Chappell as a captain. For, like Illingworth, Chappell was a player's captain. He would stick up for them thick and thin at press conferences or in any dealings with the Australian Cricket Board and he would never deviate from his position under any amount of pressure.

It's interesting to ponder how someone like Bob Massie would be faring right now if he had played all his cricket under Ian Chappell. His bowling for Australia against the World XI in Australia and against us in England was something out of this world. Nobody could ever forget his 16-wicket haul at Lord's in his Test debut, that was unbelievably brilliant.

Massie's major successes were under Chappell; he seemed to get the best out of him. I have no doubts that if he was playing under Chappell today he'd still at least be playing first-class cricket.

The Chappell magic was never better underlined than in the West Indies in 1973, when without Dennis Lillee and off-spinner Ashley Mallett, who would have thrived on those turning wickets, Chappell led Australia to victory. His front-line speed men were Max Walker, a proven workhorse, and Jeff Hammond, who blossomed under the Chappell mantle. It takes a great captain to bring off a victory like that.

Chappell's also pulled off some seemingly lost Tests and turned them into wins. The third Test against Pakistan at Sydney and the third Test at Port of Spain in Trinidad against the Windies were cliff-hanging victories from nothing but trouble.

I don't think Chappell was a genius on the field, certainly not as tactically brilliant as Illingworth, but he's used what he's had magnificently. It's been all his own doing, just for getting the players to that high pitch he must be highly praised. In that area there's no way he can be faulted.

The way he quickly moulded any new players into the side made for a very happy team rich in team spirit. That's always hard to beat, even more so when it's talented. I know that it goes with Australian cricketers and any player worth his salt for that matter, but never, ever will you see an Aussie side give in. Under Chappell they lost the first two Tests in England in 1972, but it took until the sixth Test the following series for us to get up again and he didn't have Jeff Thomson for the entire Test or Dennis Lillee after only seven overs. That's a great record, one I'd be happy to own.

But it's Chappell's non-conformity that has caused the problems which hastened his retirement as Test captain. There would have been times when it would have been a lot easier on himself to agree with any Board decisions, but the first thing he asked himself was how would that affect the players. If the answer was not in their best interests, then Chappell would fight to the death.

His method gained Aussie Test players a hundred-per-cent Test match increase from $200 to $400, and I venture to say that wouldn't have come about unless Chappell had stuck to his guns. I also believe Chappell liked the Australian image, and wanted John Citizen to recognise him as an Australian cricket captain he could associate himself with.

When we went out to toss at Lord's in my first game as England's Test captain I wore my England blazer, for I believe that's the right thing to do. Chappell didn't, and on the way out he said, 'Hey Greigy, what are you trying to do, show me up?' When I replied that what he did was his business, he said, 'That's right mate'.

Happy Indians at *Lord's* in 1974, even though they had little to enthuse about throughout the series

Below

Eknath Solkar, a great little fighter for India, is closely watched by David Lloyd, and Mike Denness

Opposite page

Basil d'Oliveira *bowling his medium pacers with* Dennis Amiss *at the non-striker's end*

Keith Boyce, one of the most savage hitters of the
ball in first-class cricket

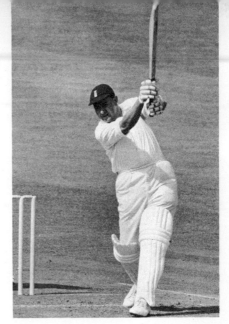

Colin Cowdrey, *aristocrat and perfect gentleman*

Even at Headingley, when the wicket was hacked about so much that play was abandoned on the last day with the game in a cliff-hanging situation, Chappell came to the ground wearing casual clothes and thongs. It didn't matter to him that worldwide television would see him in that gear. That was the way Ian Chappell wanted to dress and that was that. More often than not you'll see him in a tracksuit or tee shirt and his players followed suit. So many people were incensed at his attitude, but that could never take away the umpteen credits Chappell gained on the field.

Conformity has had repercussions over the years, but the one that sticks foremost in my mind was the then Len Hutton's appointment as England's captain in the fifties. There was a hell of a lot of controversy because he was the first professional captain of England at a time not long after professional and amateur players came out different gates.

So to Ray Illingworth and Ian Chappell I can say I've learned a lot. Not everything they've done has been right with me, but they have taught me so many points that they are surely the two top captains of my time.

South Africa's Ali Bacher had a golden run as captain, leading a team chock full of talent. It's difficult to really judge a captain under those circumstances. He took over towards the end of Peter Pollock's career, yet there were youngsters like Barry Richards, Mike Procter and Lee Irvine coming through to mould in with the experienced Graeme Pollock and Eddie Barlow. Basically they were quite a wild bunch of blokes from all the different corners of South Africa. But there was only one man who could have handled them all and that was Ali Bacher, He did a tremendous job.

The only problem in such a great side was to get them firing all together. There was a lot of speculation at one stage as to whether Bacher deserved his place in the side. Yet even though he was an untidy-looking player, he was a lot better than most people gave him credit for. He had a hard road going in at number three, following Richards or Barlow. It didn't matter which one got out, you could bet the other was firing on all six. Batting in that situation was very difficult, especially if the remaining opener got out first, for in came Graeme Pollock to tear into the attack. You can have that all on your own as the big squeeze play. He really had his work cut out trying to justify his position. Tactically he was a deep thinker and, as a doctor, obviously he was a highly intelligent man.

Having said all that—and I've said it before—Barlow would have made a great name for himself under those conditions. He's in the mould of Chappell and Illingworth, possibly more like Chappell because he does what he thinks is right and hang the consequences. It was said at the time when Bacher was captain that Barlow was the best vice-captain in the world. He'd performed well in that capacity for the Rest of the World in England. He was the sort of bloke who bubbled all over, never stopped chatting to the captain, was never shy about making any number of points, and had all sorts of ideas that were channelled through.

It's interesting to note here that Illingworth, Chappell and Barlow are all all-rounders, of a sort. Chappell's the least active as a bowler,

Garry Sobers *brings up his 200 at Melbourne off Terry Jenner*

Garry Sobers and Rohan Kanhai *both felt the axe as West Indies skippers*

but he's told me many times that whatever leg spinning he's done has given him a greater understanding of bowlers.

Of all the Test captains of my time, India's Ajit Wadekar has had one of the roughest times. Anyone who leads India has a very difficult job. While the side is winning, the captain and players are hero-worshipped. Lose, and the dream world crashes all around you.

After India had beaten the West Indies and England—the latter in India and in England—then came to England again, where they copped a mother and father of a hiding, Wadekar and the manager didn't go home for months. Wadekar stayed in England and the manager went off the the middle of Africa until the heat was off. Many of the players' homes were stoned and Wadekar's family was threatened—nothing's worth that.

Unless you're a strong character and a really top-notch player like the Nawab of Pataudi, who was way ahead of the bunch, you're courting a hard time when the wheels come off. Yet Ajit probably had more success than any other captain in the country's history. India has ridden on the shoulders of four world-class spinners for so long with a brittle batting array and a good fielding side.

So Wadekar did it tough. It's a terrible comedown from being met at Bombay airport by countless thousands who have waited for hours to staying humiliated in England. He wasn't in the top bracket by any means as a captain, but he did a good job for his country under trying circumstances and played quite a few class innings under the same pressure.

When I first went to Sussex the Nawab was captain and I believe he's still the best captain

India's had in my time—'Tiger' by name and tiger by nature. I also maintain he's the best batsman out of India in that period, despite the loss of an eye. Admittedly he has now retired again, but I view that as lack of interest these days rather than any lack of ability. If he was keen enough—and he's had years of big cricket—it wouldn't be too hard for him to dome back to near his best.

Venkat led the side to the Prudential World Cup and now Bishen Bedi's taken over. Neither has held the reins long enough for me to make any comment. Sufficient to say that Bishen is a thinking cricketer and now he's in charge he'll make a good fist of it. He's a byword in India and I can only hope he is successful, for those many friends he has at the moment may not want to know him as a losing leader, it's all happened before.

Now to the man I've already praised as my benefactor, Sir Garfield Sobers. Right in the beginning of this book I said cricketers are basically entertainers. By the time I came on the scene, Sobers was so obsessed with that line of thinking that it brought him many critics. I can't knock that, it's a brave man who can go against the accepted way of cricket life because of his beliefs. Losing Test matches with declarations is the bravest of the lot, others think it lunacy. Tactically there could well have been flaws in his captaincy, but he was such a great player that more often than not he'd rectify any mistake on his own, either by smashing out a century, grabbing a couple of vital wickets, or snapping up a catch here and there.

Sobers cannot really be bracketed with any other Test captain. He was a freak player who literally led from the front and it really didn't

Clive Lloyd, *now West Indies captain, in a minor role bowling to Greg Chappell at Brisbane 1975*

matter what he decided on from the player's point of view, or the team in general, most times it came out right because of him alone.

Now Clive Lloyd leads the mighty Windies, a fine bloke and one of the most elegant movers in the game. What's more important, Lloyd has the respect of the entire team because of his ability as a player and his standing as a man. I predict Lloyd will lead West Indies for a long time if he wants to. Although it's early days for him, he has all the ingredients to do extremely well.

In between these players was Rohan Kanhai, who led the side for a year or two, beating us well in England, losing to Australia in the West Indies and squaring the return series with England, also in the West Indies. Kanhai never really came to grips with the captaincy, despit being a fine player. There was too much in-fighting to allow him free rein and it obviously told in the end.

Having played so much County cricket in England, perhaps Kanhai's thinking was more along English lines than the happy-go-lucky West Indies style. He became safety-first, rather than debonair. Whatever the reason, Kanhai didn't remain long at the top, and the political situation, cricket-wise, could well have cost him his place in the side to Australia under Lloyd. His ability was not in question. After all, he topped the County averages and at the time of selection for Australia was averaging 330 for Warwickshire. He must have been an asset to Lloyd's side in Australia.

Captaining Pakistan can be a strange and risky affair, as Intikhab Alam and Majid Khan know so well. Both have been sacked as skipper at short notice and in circumstances that seem mysterious to an outsider. Intikhab

When success is sweet: *Kanhai waves to a deliriously happy West Indian crowd at Lord's in 1973 after beating England in the three-Test series*

was told of his demotion while play was in progress during a Test match in New Zealand. That must have been a sickening day for a fellow such as Intikhab, who always manages to appear happy and jovial and who did far more for Pakistan than many people give him credit for. It was Inti who rounded up the Pakistanis and moulded them into a tremendous fighting unit. They are a tough side to beat now and whether Majid or the latest leader Asif Iqbal leads the side to success, it can all be directed back to Intikhab Alam. Inti is the opposite to Majid, a very quiet man and also a very moody player, yet at the same time he is one of the best batsmen in the world when the mood suits him.

Asif I've mentioned before, as yet untried in Test cricket, although he was appointed Pakistan captain for the Prudential World Cup with Majid in the side and Inti out altogether. After the first game against Australia at Headingley, which Pakistan lost, Asif dropped out for a minor operation and again Majid took over. It seems musical chairs are the go in Pakistan, but the music isn't easy to listen to. Inti plays for Surrey, now led by John Edrich, and learned a lot from Mickey Stewart who was a top-rate captain when Inti first arrived. So he has had a good grounding.

Leading New Zealand is also a tough job, yet under Bevan Congdon the New Zealanders went very close to becoming a Test threat. Not since the days of John Reid had New Zealand looked good, but Congdon's efforts in my time have been great, under the circumstances. And it was all Bevan Congdon the batsman, the all-rounder and captain that made it possible. I admire the way he overcame a fearful crack on the jaw from John

Snow that resulted in a badly swollen face when New Zealand was chasing over 400 to win against England in the last innings.

Congdon shrugged off the injury and went on to make 170 as New Zealand fell only 50 runs short. That underlined his fighting spirit and the incident really summed the man up. In one way Congdon was as hard as nails, yet off the field he was quietly spoken and gained his relaxation by playing the trumpet. One side of him seemed hard to match with the other. Yet he served New Zealand with distinction.

Now Glen Turner has the captaincy. Mainly because of the talent available to him he will have his work cut out to better what Congdon has done. Turner works hard on his own game and maybe some of that will rub off on the players, but his predecessor has a big lead when it comes to captains who have made their mark for life. Bevan Congdon's a great bloke, and it's been a pleasure to do battle with him.

In another way I feel sorry for Turner. He'll lose many stalwarts shortly, those sound players who followed Congdon in the successful period. Many are reaching retirement and with so little international cricket facing New Zealand, it'll be hard to regather forces.

So, back to England and where I came in. I want to make a point of saying a sincere thank you to the man I followed as captain, Mike Denness. And if that sounds odd let me tell you I felt nothing but sympathy for Mike during the living hell that he must have gone through. He took criticism from all sides during his spell in charge. We could not go anywhere without the name Mike Denness getting a verbal working over. In the end,

It was a good day *this time for Sussex and Chris Waller agrees too*

although I am sure Mike would never admit it, he must have thought 'Thank God it's all over'.

Mike Denness as a captain always had my wholehearted support. As a man, he was someone I liked and trusted. I played in every Test he captained and I still maintain that the stick should not have been aimed at him. All right, he had little success. We were lucky to escape with a drawn series on the 1973 to 1974 West Indies trip and we took a hammering from the Australians the next year. By the time the 1975 season began with that innings defeat against the Aussies at Edgbaston most cricket followers had already lined up Mike's head on the chopping block.

All I can say is, I am glad it wasn't me in his shoes. Mike was made captain at a time when our fortunes were low. The England old guard were disappearing from the scene and we were left with a mightly rebuilding job. Mike, who was not even an established Test player himself, may soon have felt he was out of his depth, but through all the agonies he must have endured, he still managed to hold his head up. Man, he must have been lonely. But

he is a good bloke and I would love to see Denness land a return to the England side as a batsman in his own right, and succeed.

I'd like specially to mention two other captains of England, poles apart individually, yet successful in their own way—Colin Cowdrey, the aristocrat and perfect gentleman on and off the field, and Brian Close, the tough, kind, hard, stubborn Yorkshireman. Both served England well, Cowdrey ever so gentlemanly and one who never made an enemy the world over, Close the general who cracked a side into line, fearing no one, caring not if he trod heavily on toes from the top to the bottom. In their various ways I admired them both.

After running through so many captains from various countries, it is obvious there's no set pattern to follow. Each had his own particular leadership qualities and some will go down in history as giants forever. At worst the others can safely say 'I've captained my country in Test cricket'. That honour falls to the very fortunate few and I'm grateful to be one of them.

10

The Men in Support

The Fielders

Catches win matches, runs saved in the field are bonus runs you don't have to get. Chestnut sayings for sure, but so very true.

The men in support are split into outfielders and 'coppers', those close to the wicket. I don't have to think about my top outfielder, he readily springs to mind—South Africa's Colin Bland. What a fieldsman! Here was a man dedicated to practice, hours and hours of it, and he was blessed with uncanny anticipation. Naturally, he was also agile and very fit, obviously prerequisites for an outfielder who could still be as brilliant towards the end of the day as he was at the start.

Practice was foremost in his mind. I believe that on a farm in Rhodesia he set up a hockey net and a stump that was spring-loaded. He would get a few of the young lads working on the farm to throw ball after ball at him, making him run all the time from one side to the other, and he'd pick up and throw as fast as he could at that solitary stump.

The boys were as safe as a bank. They used to wander around the side of the net, knowing full well that Bland's bullet-like returns would invariably hit or just miss the stump, then crash into the net. This would go on for three to four hours a day mind you, every day he wasn't playing. If that's not utter dedication I don't know what is.

So Colin Bland made his great arm even greater. His accuracy was like radar and his anticipation so magnificent that it almost looked as though the ball conveniently jumped into his hand. That wasn't so. He could read what would happen to the ball as it sped across the turf. How often have you seen a good fieldsman get a rap on the wrist as the ball hops just as he's picking it up? It never

happened to Bland, he seemed to know it would hop and was ready for it. Bland had a novel theory in the field, he walked in with the bowler but remained stationary when the batsman played his shot. Ever since I can remember I was taught to walk in with the bowler, and therefore be on the move when the shot was played.

Bland contends you must be off balance doing that, or at worst be on the wrong foot and unable to change direction quickly enough. He'd watch the batsman like a hawk, see which way his ball was coming, then set off, and he was right on the spot. That's what made him such a dangerous cover field in particular, and was one of the reasons why he so often was left to patrol all the area from point to mid-off—he did it on his ear.

I vividly recall watching Geoff Boycott and Ken Barrington batting together at Port Elizabeth in South Africa during a Test match. Boycott played a solid shot through cover well to Bland's right, and called. Barrington got about three yards down the wicket before Boycott screamed out, 'No'. By the time Barrington had propped and dived for safety, Bland's rocket return had shattered the stumps at the bowler's end. A magnificent piece of fielding, but an everyday occurrence to Colin Bland. Barrington was safe, by the skin of his teeth, but next ball struck by Boycott even further to Bland's right didn't interest Barrington, who turned his back on Boycott's call for a run.

To prove Bland's pin-point accuracy was no fluke, when South Africa's game against Kent at Canterbury a few years back was washed out one day, the television cameras stayed there. On national television Bland was asked

History is made as Ian Chappell becomes the first Australian non-keeper to take 100 Test catches. The batsman was Lawrence Rowe

Great photo, muffed chance. *Shafiq Ahmad and Majid Khan between them spill Keith Fletcher at Headingley, 1974*

to give an exhibition to see how many throws it would take to knock all three stumps out of the ground. It took three. The first from forty yards out and on the run wiped out two, the second from the same distance banged into keeper Denis Lindsay's gloves right above the stump, the third saw Lindsay diving for safety as Bland smashed number three stump out of the ground.

It was an incredible display for those who rarely saw him and just another experience for those who had seen him do it countless times. In cold, hard fact Colin Bland was worth possibly 50 to 60 runs each innings, runs saved through his sheer genius. He could field in the slips but was rarely wasted there. He was a very handy batsman who gave the nice feeling of being those 50 to 60 runs in front before he even took guard. That was his priceless value to South Africa and Rhodesia.

Two more recent Test fielding greats and the closest to Bland are West Indian Clive Lloyd and Australia's Paul Sheahan. Lloyd has the same incredible ability to hit the stumps often, whereas Sheahan was superbly accurate, but a man who found the keeper's gloves rather than the wood. Rarely did he let the keeper wander more than a skip away from the wicket.

On the ground, both shared the same type of anticipation as Bland, the ball losing itself snugly into their safe hands, but neither could have matched what to me was the greatest piece of fielding I've ever seen. It was at Bloemfontain in South Africa in a Gillette Cup game where Bland dived full-length to his right in the covers, rolled over in a somersault and before he'd stopped rolling had rocketed a return back to the keeper, over the bails.

That took my breath away, and while Lloyd and Sheahan have been head and shoulders above everyone else in recent years, they couldn't consistently match Bland, although both were faster on foot over a longer distance. Lloyd is strong, immensely so, with long arms that look like a scoop as he races across the field. Sheahan is gazelle-like, showing all the prowess that made him a schoolboy athletic champion. They both make it look so easy. Without doubt they are the best in their era.

Just behind comes Asif Iqbal, lightning fast in the field, with a safe pair of hands and a strong arm from thirty yards out. Over a greater distance he couldn't match Lloyd or Sheahan, but he saved many runs for Pakistan.

No outfielder's story would be complete without mentioning Australia's dogged Ross Edwards. If ever a man made himself into something he wasn't born to like the others, Edwards was that man. He wasn't quick in the field, didn't have an arm like any of the others I've mentioned, but for sheer tenacity he took some beating. I've seen him with padding over both elbows from grass burns after diving headlong to save the odd run, seen him grovelling in wet and dry conditions, even dive towards a concrete fence, stop the ball in full flight, bounce off the wall and return it. Again only to save one. But they all add up. Nobody could have tried harder than Ross Edwards for his side in the field and he saved plenty.

The Nawab of Pataudi, although small in stature, also rates highly among the outfielders of my time. He too was cat-like, very similar to Lloyd, and had a good arm.

The one to watch, and time will tell if he

One that got away. *Rod Marsh doesn't miss many,*
but this one from Lawrence Rowe off Gary
Gilmour was just too far away and Marsh spilled it,
Brisbane, 1975

Overleaf

Deryck Murray: *the West Indian keeper is always a*
thorn in any bowler's side

Clive Lloyd: *his fielding takes my breath away*

gets close to Bland, is the West Indies' Vivi Richards, an exciting prospect. He's very much the newcomer to Test cricket, yet he showed in the Prudential World Cup final at Lord's against Australia that he's potentially something out of the box. He found the stumps with three magnificent throws from almost side on to account for three of Australia's five run-outs. It takes something extra special to do that consistently. Bland did it, can Richards emulate him?

When you talk about outfielders, West Indians always come to mind. Keith Boyce isn't a fast mover in the field, for he does a lot of bowling, but when he gets that ball in his hands, beware. I always feel sorry for any bowler having to take his outfield return, for it's flat, hard and accurate. If it's a bit high on occasions there had better be a host of fielders backing it or it'll take a couple of hops and crash into the fence on the other side of the field.

West Indians seem to have arms made of steel and sinew and never suffer from tennis-elbow type injuries as we do. So there are any amount of West Indians who do a good job in this area, I've mentioned only the best of them.

Saving runs in the outfield is vital, but the 'coppers' are the reflex men who can turn the trend of a game by snapping up a seemingly impossible catch in the close cordon. Graham Roope hasn't played many Test matches for England, but to me he's the best slips catcher in the world today. Running him a very close second would be Australia's Greg Chappell, such a complete fielding all-rounder he would rate anywhere in close or in the outfield. If I had to pick two chaps for my side

they'd be the two I'd go for and they could take either slip.

They have diametrically opposite ways of catching the ball. Roope prefers to get down low, accepting the chance like a baseball catcher with fingers pointing upwards and cupped to his chest. Chappell, like all the Australians, has his hands tucked into his stomach, leaving the hands pointed down. Ian Chappell once told me that former captain Bobby Simpson, also a champion slip fielder, had taught the Australians to slip field in that fashion.

Simpson was different again. He preferred on occasions to let the ball hit him on the chest and then clutch it safely. Sounds a bit bruising to me, I wouldn't relish taking a hot one off Dennis Lillee or Jeff Thomson in the Simpson way, but it worked well for him so it can't be bad.

Techniques obviously vary, but it's whether or not the catch is taken that counts, how doesn't matter. Great slip fielders like Roope and Greg Chappell take them everywhere—high, low and on either side. I can't really remember any particular catch either has made, I just expect them to catch the lot. It's the rare one they drop that sticks in your mind.

Judgement depends on how highly you rate a slip fielder. England's Keith Fletcher can be safe, but is unspectacular. When he takes a fantastic catch I remember it, it's all relative.

In his heyday Colin Cowdrey was also brilliant. His reflexes were so fast he often caught the ball and whipped it into his pocket before anyone had a chance to work out where the ball was. Even the crowd would be baffled when they saw the batsman walking

The Aussies are great 'coppers'. *Proof enough in this graphic shot of Rick McCosker accepting a hot one, watched by the gleeful trio of Ian Chappell, Ian Redpath and Greg Chappell, Brisbane, 1975*

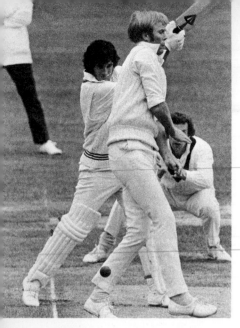

I like it there. The only danger area is between the ankles and thighs. Here John Parker tries to remove me, watched by a crouching David Lloyd, at Lord's, 1973

Next page

Ray Illingworth *takes another brilliant catch from close range to dismiss Paul Sheahan at Headingley 1972. The slip is Peter Parfitt and keeper Alan Knott*

out after slipping into a cover drive, but they didn't know where the ball was either. Kipper would walk down the wicket, patting the bowler on the head in recognition, and then the penny would drop, he'd nicked it into his trouser pocket.

Ian Chappell's another top-class slip fielder, but it's asking a lot to captain a side, be thinking all the time, yet concentrating in this vital area. That's probably why he's spilled a few, but then he's taken a lot.

Gully is another specialist position. I've always maintained you can watch the ball from first to third slip right from the bowler's hand, from there to gully you've only got time to watch the batsman play his stroke. In Australia there are two champion gullys, Ashley Mallett and Ian Redpath. Against us in Australia last tour these two brought off some of the most incredible catches I've ever seen and made them look so easy.

But the best I've ever seen in the gully is Sussex's Peter Graves. The catches he's taken off John Snow have been unreal. Like Roope he prefers to catch them from low down with fingers up. He reminds me of a soccer goalkeeper, snapping them up either side. Yet when you're as good as these three, there's little in it. West Indies' Lance Gibbs is another class gully man, but I've only seen him in his latter years, and can't rate him in the bracket of Graves, Mallett and Redpath.

Around the corner is another vital spot and yet another specialised position. As in so many other facets of the game, Garry Sobers gets my number one vote there. Sobers had tremendous insight into the batsman's movement. If he went back, Sobers stayed where he was. If he went forward, so too did Sobers

and therefore many of Sober's catches were made to look so easy, but he'd made them so.

Many fieldsmen who have taken on this position never laid hand on some balls in the air because they didn't have Sobers' anticipation. Being predominantly left-handed was definitely an advantage Sobers had with a right-handed batsman, with most chances going to his strongest side. India's Venkat wasn't far behind Sobers, and he also has taken many a good catch in the slip cordon.

They are really tested when it comes to the spinners. Standing back is not a piece of cake, but it is easier. That applies even more so to the forward short-leg and bat-pad positions. A few players have nearly died fielding there, after being hit on the head, especially off the spinners when there's so little time to move and protect yourself. Some can only field there for awhile, then become shell-shocked and move out to safer pastures, never to return. That makes my top man there even more special, Eknath Solkar from India.

Ekkie's far in the front of this hardy lot. One memorable catch among many I've been privileged to see Solkar take was in India and the batsman was England's captain Tony Lewis. Bedi was bowling and Solkar was virtually in Lewis' hip pocket. Lewis gave it the big sweep, got a bottom edge onto his pad and the ball just blooped down short on the leg side.

Solkar dived forward and caught it—a fantastic effort. For at some stage he must have seen the full face of Lewis' blade and known that the ball could well be travelling at full throttle over a minute distance right towards him.

Had Lewis middled it, Solkar had every

Turner protects himself. *This time Kallicharran
miscues Ashley Mallett as the ball appears to stay
on the end of his bat. Closely watched by Rod
Marsh, Brisbane 1975*

chance of being hit right between the eyes. Yet he continued to watch for the catch. Absolutely amazing. He's fielded there for quite some time and the last time I spoke to him he was starting to feel the pinch and was having second thoughts about going back there. But he's lasted far longer than most, and performed far better. Probably it's because he never protected himself, unlike Surrey's Mike Edwards, the next best I've seen in 'suicide corner'. Edwards protected himself so well that quite often he'd catch the return off his arms that were pointing to the sky in front of his face.

Talking about dangerous positions, full marks to Pakistan's Sarfraz Nawaz. When playing for his country or Northamptonshire, I've seen Sarfraz field with his left foot on the wicket edge, in loose terms a very, very short mid-wicket. With his long arms he can stretch out and touch the bat. Yet he's fielded there for all and sundry, in an ideal position to be swatted out of business. Many people have said I field in a dangerous position, close and square on the off side, but it's far more peaceful there than where Sarfraz stands. He's classed as an irritating sort of fielder, he just stares at you. You are very conscious of him being there, you can hear him breathing. That makes a lot of batsmen fidgety and has caused the downfall of most of them.

As for my position, I know I can only be hit from my ankles to about the middle of my thighs, for I'll always turn side on if I reckon I'm in strife. My sole purpose, in many ways like Sarfraz, is to make a batsman do something stupid to remove me, and many's the time he's been caught in the cordon. A batsman doesn't see the bat-pad man, but

Sarfraz and I are in a spot where it's a constant visual reminder.

There have been times when I've inadvertantly upset a bowler by fielding so close. Derek Underwood was one. He was so afraid to bowl a loose ball in case I got cleaned up that he froze, literally froze. That's when I am likely to cop one, and there's no doubt it can hurt, but it can't kill me. During the tour of India last time I picked up Sunny Gavaskar twice off Derek, and that broke the ice. It took awhile for him not to worry about it, but once he got the hang of it we became a useful tandem.

I've mentioned specialised positions, but there are some players like Greg Chappell, Lloyd, Doug Walters, Abid Ali, Sobers and Chris Old who can field anywhere and do it justice. They are very special team members.

There must be some connection between class slips men and top order batsmen. Every one of my slips fieldmen comes into that category, and I haven't mentioned Barry Richards and Rohan Kanhai, who are both fine slip fielders.

Richards is very like Greg Chappell, but far more casual. As I said of his batting, Richards, without the pull of Test cricket to retain interest, has obviously never reached the heights he's capable of in the cordon. He often fields with hands on hips or knees, and when the chance presents itself snaps it up. Kanhai's greying hair belies his speed as a slip fielder—even now.

On an overall basis the two best fielding sides I've run into have got to be India and Australia. India in India was unreal. As their attack was centred on spin, there were five in keeper Engineer, Wadekar at slip, Venkat and

Opposite page

A mighty hot one. *Rick McCosker takes a one-
handed catch to dismiss Alan Knott off a searing
Jeff Thomson full toss at Edgbaston in 1975.
Defending himself is Doug Walters. Greg Chappell
and Gary Gilmour look on*

Not out. *Gloucester's Jim Foat just beats me to the
punch at Lord's, 1973*

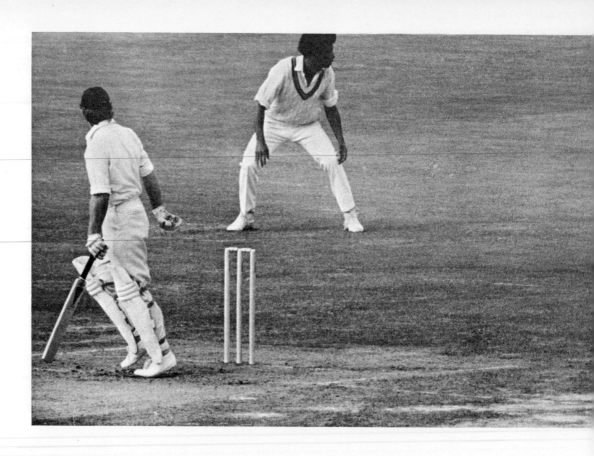

Graham Roope, *the best slips man I've seen,
proves the point by catching Ken Wadsworth off
Geoff Arnold at Trent Bridge in 1973, as Keith
Fletcher and Alan Knott watch the result with
interest*

The agility of Sobers. Here he dives in front and across Rohan Kanhai to catch Dennis Amiss off Keith Boyce at Lord's in 1973. At left is Bernard Julien, keeper Deryck Murray and short leg Roy Fredericks

Below

Vivian Richards, the latest in a long line of superb West Indian fieldsmen, makes the first of his three run-outs in the 1975 Prudential World Cup final at Lord's. Victim Alan Turner is watched by an engrossed Deryck Murray

A memorable catch *and Eknath Solkar wraps up*
Tony Lewis, much to the delight of Erapalli
Prasanna and keeper Farokh Engineer

A good feeling. *I manage to stop a John Edrich cut*
at Worcester during the 1974 Test trial, but
couldn't stop his century

Abid Ali around the corner, and Solkar at bat-pad. The pressure was intense, you'd dare not nick one, in fact middling the ball presented the only safety from their bucket-like hands.

The Aussies last tour had some unreal support of blitzmen in Lillee and Thomson. First of all there was Ross Edwards saving run after run in covers, a cordon of Marsh, two Chappells, Walters, McCosker, Redpath and Mallett catching ninety eight per cent of what was flying around, and even a man like Walker, who wouldn't have the nickname of 'Tangles' unless he was a little clumsy, crabbing seemingly uncatchable balls out of the air.

They all created misery for us there, anything that left the ground at more than paper thickness height was snapped up cleanly. Even at that height we weren't too sure it wouldn't be taken, so magnificent a fielding display did they turn in.

If I just wanted to watch outfielders I'd watch the West Indies. They have the flair, flat arms, and they're fast around the field. Say the game changed and you had to pick all outfielders, the bulk of them would come from the West Indies.

That leaves only England, where it's a completely different game altogether. Because it's a fully professional game and therefore the players' average age is far older than in other countries, the mobility isn't there. So for a start we are handicapped.

I'm not making any excuses for English fielding at times because we have had some tremendous days. But basically, over an extended period, we could not compete with the other countries.

It gets to the stage where, come selection time, for one place you may be faced with a less mobile, but very experienced player or settle on an inexperienced player because of his ability to field well and his mobility. The one-day game however has made a huge improvement in the fielding department in England. I don't know what the answer is, it's a difficult one to overcome.

One thing for sure, when I arrived in England I had a good, strong arm. I couldn't understand why players were bowling the ball in from the outfield, right from the start of the season. I soon found out. It's so bitterly cold in that period it's very easy to throw your arm out, and have to carry it through seven-day-a-week cricket for six months. Nothing's worth that, it makes for a hellishly long and painful summer. Gradually when it warms up you can get back to normal arms, but always warily. Taking a hot slip catch early on is nerve-racking. You might take it all right, but you know about it for the rest of the day, sometimes longer.

So fielding's not an easy part of the game, but anywhere, anytime, in any game, it can make the difference between winning and losing. The best sides have the best fielding lineups, there's proof enough in that.

11

Tony Greig's World XI

Cricket the world over is on the up. Interest is at an all-time high and there are openings galore for any youngster who wants to make it to the top. But, as you can see from my list of greats, the road isn't easy. It takes time and a lot of hard work.

For those who are impatient, I advise them to ease up and take stock of what's in store, set their sights on a goal and then step by step make sure they put it all together to achieve it. If any player isn't prepared to do that and wants it handed to him on a platter he should give it away and forget it. That type of player isn't worth having around. He becomes a drag on team-mates and lowers morale. Every country vitally requires depth, it's the life-blood of the game. Some are better off than others, but over a period it generally works out reasonably even.

The future is so bright, on and off the field. One-day cricket is here to stay and will blend in well with the three, four and five-day game. That's been so successfully proved in England and normally what is successful there eventually finds a similar level in all the other countries.

One-day cricket improves fielding and running between wickets and teaches bowlers to bowl to their field. But there are problems. Middle-order batsmen—and they are generally the younger brigade—have to move quicker into gear, far faster than if they had time to build an innings, and spinners take a back seat unless they can adjust to being economical. But overall, it's a necessary adjunct to the game, a saviour when it comes to sponsorship and therefore means more money in the game generally as well as in the players' pockets.

Yet Test cricket will always be the ultimate team game. Being classed as a great is the highest pinnacle an individual can achieve.

So I want to select my World XI, a seemingly impossible task but an interesting exercise. From the outset I ran into problems. How do you leave out the two best captains in the world, Illingworth and Ian Chappell? How do you fit Dennis Lillee, Mike Procter, Andy Roberts, Jeff Thomson and John Snow into the one side?

Those were just a couple of insurmountable decisions, so for better or worse, the top team of my era is:

BARRY RICHARDS

GEOFF BOYCOTT

CLIVE LLOYD

GARRY SOBERS (Captain)

GRAEME POLLOCK

MIKE PROCTER

ALAN KNOTT

JOHN SNOW

ANDY ROBERTS

BISHEN BEDI

CHANDRASEKHAR

What a side!
It would be unbeatable, with immense strength in every department. But there are many left who could provide stiff opposition.

The end of the greatest innings as Garry Sobers leaves the MCG after his magnificent 254 for the Rest of the World against Australia

It would be sensational if my World Second XI met them on a good cricketing wicket.
Eddie Barlow

Colin Cowdrey

Ian Chappell (Captain)

Greg Chappell

Rohan Kanhai

Basil D'Oliveira

Rod Marsh

Intikhab Alam

Jeff Thomson

Dennis Lillee

Lance Gibbs

With all twenty-two players at the peak of their careers this would be a spectacular clash before huge crowds and a fitting tribute to the greatest game on earth.

127

Trent Bridge, 1973. *Graham Roope dives to catch
New Zealand's Glenn Turner off Geoff Arnold*

Height helps. *I make the most of being six foot seven*